RUBBING ELBOWS
WITH ROYALTY

Volume Two: A Commentary on the
Life of David from Second Samuel

SPARKY PRITCHARD

Mile-Hi Publishers, Inc. • Denver, Colorado 80226

Acknowledgments

Many friends have contributed to the publication of this work. To these I wish to express my deepest gratitude in making a dream become reality.

The secretarial and production team have been invaluable in proofreading, typesetting, corrections, and layout. I thank Marilyn Danley, Terri Janke, Irene Gorham, and Patsy Southwell for their efforts.

The creativity of Chuck Renstrom and Linda Anderson in producing the cover photo and cover design respectively is irreplaceable.

Nancy Bundy has sacrifically given of her time in typing the revised manuscript. Words are inadequate to tell how much I appreciate what she has done.

Special thanks go to Guyla Nelson, who has unselfishly given of her time to read and offer helpful suggestions relating to this final manuscript. Without her thoughtful, careful guidance, this book would never be. And to my wife, Kathy, I say "thank you" for proofreading the text and encouraging me along the way.

Finally, I wish to express my appreciation to Dr. Ed Nelson, my pastor and my father-in-law, who has had a great influence on my ministry. Thanks for your consistent, godly example to me and to preachers everywhere.

*Affectionately dedicated
to my parents,
George and Joan Pritchard,
whose sacrifice, love,
and encouragement
continue to bless
my life.*

Foreword

The study of the Life of David is thrilling and challenging to any serious Bible student. These chapters in this book were first written to lead the adult classes in South Sheridan Baptist Church as we studied II Samuel and the life of David.

As I studied and taught these lessons, I was greatly blessed. Because of the blessing I received, I am quite confident that the people in my class also were blessed. I can say that these messages have been proved in the crucible of the classroom.

The author has done an outstanding job in preparing these chapters. They will be a help to the pastor, to the Sunday School worker, and to the students who spend time in II Samuel.

Read these chapters. You will walk with David. You will weep with him. You will learn lessons and principles for your life as a child of God.

I am confident that the author will lead you down the thrilling paths of David's life just as I have been. I commend these chapters to you as that which will help you live to honor the Lord.

Dr. Ed Nelson, Pastor
South Sheridan Baptist Church

Denver, Colorado

Preface

David—the name is as melodic as the songs which flowed from his pen. His life, in contrast, was not always harmonic. If you should recall the most memorable events of his life, two would probably come to mind—an incident involving a sling (with Goliath) and an incident involving a fling (with Bathsheba).

Here was a man who could conquer one giant but fell helplessly before another. One day he was on top of the world; the next, in the valley of discouragement. He was strong in his political life but weak in his family life—a capable administrator but an insensitive father. Frequently, David was a "rock" of stability; but often he was a "stone of stumbling."

We can see him pursuing God's ideal but also yielding to selfish desires. Far from perfect, David struggles where we struggle. Therein lies our identity with him.

This commentary on Second Samuel is essentially a biography of David's life, covering approximately forty years, from the destruction of Ziklag to the purchase of the threshingfloor of Araunah near the end of his reign. Originally, these studies were written for the Adult

Bible Study Classes of the South Sheridan Baptist Church where Dr. Ed Nelson is pastor. Because of the encouragement of Dr. Nelson, the congregation, and other friends, this material was expanded and refined into the current format. Although the research was thorough, I have endeavored to make the text clear, simple, and practical. To this end each chapter concludes with a synopsis of basic principles to be learned from David's successes and failures.

Two years ago I began a journey with David. We traveled along dusty paths in the Judean desert and huddled in dark recesses of musty caves. I have protested his bad decisions and applauded his good ones. I have laughed with him, conquered with him, hurt with him, and cried with him. My life is richer, having rubbed elbows with David. My prayer is that yours will be, too.

Sparky Pritchard
Denver, 1983

Contents

Surveying Second Samuel

It's a good thing daddies have children; it gives them an opportunity to buy all the toys the dad has always wanted to play with. The day after Christmas an ad in the local paper caught my eye. "The toy that every child wants at a price everyone can afford!" Tossing the paper aside, I told my wife that I was going out and would return in a few minutes. (Someone ought to award purple hearts to the brave souls who venture out to the malls on the day after Christmas.) Buying a special present for your kids ought to be fun, or so I thought. Driving to a nearby mall, I circled the parking lot for some time looking for a parking place. That was fun!? Then I fought through the crowds to find the "special" I wanted. More fun!? Don't forget the long line to get to the cashier. Oh, what fun!? In a few moments I was outside, experiencing a strange sensation—fresh air! I was able to breathe again. Freedom at

last! At least, until I pulled my car into the traffic leading out of the shopping center. Three or four traffic
lights later I was out onto the main street. Boy, this is
really fun!? Amazingly, I made it home before my wife
called the police to file a Missing Persons Report. When
the girls saw the bag, they knew it was a gift. Fatigued
but happy, I presented my girls with two new Rubik's
Cubes. Of course, I had to play with—I mean demonstrate—the cube first. Figuring this thing out would be
a snap. After all, I had seen little kids solving the patterns. An hour passed—and alas, no solution. I couldn't
even complete one side (but my daughter could). I think
I'm beginning to suffer from the Charlie Brown complex. Good grief!

One thing I did observe about the cube. Make one
false move and you're a goner! The harder you try, the
worse the cube gets.

Life is a lot like the Rubik's Cube. It begins innocently
enough; but given time and a few ill-advised turns, you
have a mess on your hands.

David must have felt somewhat like that in the latter
chapters of I Samuel. He had made a few wrong turns.
You might call it the zigzag at Ziklag, but David learned
a wise lesson. He put his mess in God's hands. Little by
little, the proper patterns began to form.

The first ten chapters of II Samuel record the
triumphs of David as all the pieces fall into place. But
when David takes matters into his own hands again in
chapter eleven, he blows it. The remaining chapters tell
the troubles he encountered because of his transgres-
sions. His "cube" surely did get messed up.

The book of II Samuel was probably compiled by
Nathan and Gad sometime after 931 B.C., the date
marking the division of the kingdom. The book covers
the period of approximately forty and one-half years of

David's reign (1011-971 B.C.). As I Samuel focused on the kingdom of Israel established, II Samuel focuses on the kingdom of Israel extended through the conquests of David. Being a biography, the book naturally divides itself into three periods of the king's life.

In order that we might know where we are heading, let's make a brief overview of these segments in the life of David.

The Successes of David (II Samuel 1—10)

Israel's first king, Saul, had been slain on the slopes of Mount Gilboa by the Philistine armies. News of Saul's death traveled quickly to Ziklag, where David and his men were clearing up the ruins of their city (Chapter 1). Upon hearing the report, David eulogized the fallen king and his friend Jonathan. Since the kingdom was in disarray over the death of Saul and defeat by the Philistines, God brought David to Hebron to be crowned king over Judah (Chapter 2). In a rival move Abner, captain of Saul's armies, placed Ishbosheth, Saul's son, in power over the northern tribes. After a brief period of civil war, Abner defected to David but was killed by the vengeful Joab (Chapter 3). Ishbosheth's assassination soon followed (Chapter 4), and David became king over all Israel (Chapter 5). In order to solidify the kingdom, the capital was moved north to Jerusalem. In placing the ark of the covenant in Jerusalem, the city was made the religious center as well (Chapter 6). The exaltation and extension of the kingdom continued through the Davidic Covenant (Chapter 7) and David's conquests (Chapters 8, 10). But even in victory, the heart of the king was still tender as he remembered his covenant with Jonathan and cared for the ailing Mephibosheth (Chapter 9).

The Sins of David (II Samuel 11—12)

Unfortunately, David's life does not go unmarred by sin. In an unguarded moment the king spied a beautiful young Jewish woman taking a bath in the evening (Chapter 11). Overcome by his own lust, he sent for Bathsheba and committed adultery. When it was learned that she was with child, he sent for her husband, who had been away fighting a battle. Being more righteous than David, he refused to spend time with his wife while his comrades fought God's enemies. Frustration and futility set in as David sent Uriah to the front line with his own death sentence sealed in a note to Joab.

David thought he had covered his sin, but God saw it and brought a message of judgment through His prophet Nathan (Chapter 12). Although God forgave David and restored him to fellowship, the consequences of the sin were forthcoming.

The Sorrows of David (II Samuel 12—24)

David's troubles began with the death of the child which Bathsheba had been carrying (Chapter 12). Then came the incestuous act of his son Amnon with Tamar (Chapter 13). In time, Amnon was murdered by Tamar's brother Absalom, who then had to flee from his father David's face. At the urging of Joab, Absalom was permitted to return to Jerusalem (Chapter 14). But an embittered Absalom began to conspire to take the kingdom from his father. David barely escaped from Jerusalem with a modest group of loyal followers (Chapter 15). Although David fled to the Transjordan area (Chapter 16), he had spies in Absalom's court. One was Hushai, who helped David by defeating the counsel of Ahithophel (Chapter 17). Inevitably, the confrontation between David and Absalom took place, with David being the victor (Chapter 18). Although David returned to Jerusalem (Chapter 19), his sorrow continued as Sheba of Benjamin led another revolt in the kingdom (Chapter 20). This was quickly dispersed by the action of the people of Abel-beth-maachah.

On the heels of this problem followed a three-year famine (Chapter 21). Chapters 22 and 23 record a song of praise by David and the acts of his mighty men. However, the final chapter concludes the book with the sin of David in numbering the people. This brought a plague on Israel that took the lives of seventy thousand men (Chapter 24).

From this brief survey of II Samuel we see vividly illustrated two principles from the pages of Scripture. Hosea wrote, *"Sow to yourselves in righteousness, reap in mercy"* *(Hosea 10:12).* David had turned back to God in I Samuel 30, and God rewarded him with success in II Samuel 1—10.

But there is another principle recorded in Hosea: *"For they have sown the wind, and they shall reap the whirlwind"* *(Hosea 8:7).* In II Samuel 11 David sowed the wind when he committed adultery. His whirlwind swept away thousands of lives and brought unrest throughout the remainder of his days.

Three thousand years have come and gone since the early days of this kingdom. Many things have changed, but God's principles have not. As we rub elbows with King David, let's learn from his mistakes as well as from his successes. Maybe we can avoid planting the wrong seeds and praying for crop failure.

TIMELESS TRUTHS FOR TODAY

1. Sow in righteousness and you shall reap in mercy.
2. Sow the wind and you shall reap a whirlwind.

Chapter 1

When the Enemy Falls
II Samuel 1:1-27

Have you ever been driving down the road at the maximum speed the law permits, only to find yourself tailgated by some guy who thinks he is an entrant in the Indy 500? He sits on his horn, flashes his lights, and jerks his car around like a poor man's Al Unser. Suddenly there comes a slight break in traffic. Putting his foot through the carburetor, within moments he is a fond memory. I have often caught myself wishing a patrolman were just over the hill. On at least two occasions my wish has been fulfilled. In a "true spirit" of love and compassion, I have smiled and waved as I passed the two vehicles stopped along the roadside. With satisfaction that justice has been done, I have driven on to my destination.

If you are honest, you have probably had the same feeling. Unfortunately, those reactions are not reserved for the highway alone. These same attitudes creep in

among God's people. How many times have you been
tempted, even yielded, to feel satisfaction over someone who has been "caught" in sin and has been forced
to pay the price? Maybe it was someone who had
wronged you, who had offended a friend, or who was
simply an unlikable character. Maybe it was someone
who did not measure up to your "list" of spirituality.

The first chapter of II Samuel places David in a pre-
carious situation. Having been chased by Saul for nearly
ten years, David was told that his old nemesis was dead.
You might expect a celebration, a triumphant feast, or
dancing in the streets. But not from David. David was
still contemplating his own failures at Ziklag. His reaction was one of remorse, not revelry.

Two great lessons can be learned from this passage.
First, our reaction to the failures of others reveals the
depth of our relationship with God. Second, when we
see our antagonists fall, we should strengthen and restore them if possible, considering our own weaknesses.

The Report of the Amalekite (1:1-10)

David had wandered far from God in deciding to ally
himself with the king of Gath and take up residence in
the village of Ziklag. On one occasion when David was
absent, Amalekites had raided Ziklag and had left it
desolate (I Samuel 30:1). This tragic event marked the
turning point of David's life (I Samuel 30:6). After
seeking God's guidance, he pursued the Amalekites and
rescued his family and friends (I Samuel 30:18). Then
David and his men returned to Ziklag and began pick-
ing up the pieces of their shattered dreams, wondering,
"What next?" On the third day after their return, a
young man approached David (II Samuel 1:1-2). Bearing the signs of mourning (i.e., *"with his clothes rent and*

earth upon his head"), he bowed in submission to the future king. David asked where he had come from. He answered, *"Out of the camp of Israel am I escaped" (1:3)*. Sensing that a calamity had taken place, David inquired further. He could hardly believe that Israel had been defeated and that many Israelites had been slain, including Saul and Jonathan (1:4). The young man related how he just happened to be walking on Mount Gilboa when he saw Saul leaning on his spear (perhaps from exhaustion). As the Philistine warriors closed in, Saul noticed the young man behind him and called him near (1:6-7). The king asked that the Amalekite kill him because *"anguish"* (Hebrew—cramps?) was come upon him. In an effort to protect himself in the eyes of David, the young Amalekite rationalized that since Saul's death was impending, he accommodated the king's request (1:10). As proof, the messenger presented Saul's bracelet and crown to David.

Was this what had really happened on the slopes of Gilboa? Does this account supply us with additional information concerning Saul's death? I think not. There are too many unanswered questions and seeming contradictions for this to be so. For instance, in I Samuel 31 the Amalekite is not presented as "finishing off" a wounded Saul. Although verse six states that Saul was leaning on his spear, it does not say that he had fallen on his spear. Nowhere is the Hebrew word for *"lean"* used for causing death. Besides, Saul had been killed by falling on a sword (I Samuel 31:4). Another inconsistency in the story is evident by comparing the Amalekite's claim to have slain Saul to the claim in I Samuel 31:5-6 that Saul killed himself. The account in I Samuel says that Saul wanted to die so that he might avoid abuse by the Philistines. The Amalekite cited Saul's desire to die as related to his present physical discomfort.

Other problem questions include: How could a person happen by chance into the middle of a heated battle? Could the Philistine chariots follow Saul up rugged Gilboa? Why would a young man walk over and talk to Saul while the archers were winging in their arrows (I Samuel 31:3)? How can we justify Saul's desiring an Amalekite, of all people, to kill him? And why did the young man not hang around and become the hero of the Philistines for killing Saul?

Obviously, the story was a fabrication. The young Amalekite, while looting the battlefield in the aftermath, came across the slain king. Taking advantage of the situation, he brought the emblems of Saul's office to David. In addition to mentioning Saul's death, he also revealed that Jonathan had died. Why did he not mention the other two sons? Jonathan was the heir to the throne (I Samuel 20:31). The way was now clear for "King" David. The young man probably thought that such news would bring a handsome reward from the soon-to-be king.

The Reaction to the News (1:11-16)

In a move which must have shocked the Amalekite, David tore his clothes (a sign of mourning). This act was immediately copied by David's men (1:11). They all *"mourned, and wept, and fasted"* until the sun went down because of the fallen king and the disastrous outcome of Gilboa (1:12).

After these hours of sorrow, David again came to see the young man, asking, "From where did you say you came?" *"I am the son of a stranger, an Amalekite" (1:13).* "Oh, another one of those!" If that Amalekite had only known the problems that the Amalekites had just caused David! David reprimanded the messenger for

killing the Lord's anointed (1:14). David had been faced
with two opportunities to kill Saul but had refrained
himself in both situations. (See I Samuel 24:3-6; 26:7-
9). As penalty for the confessed murder, David had the
Amalekite put to death (1:15). David must have believed the testimony of the man; but remember, it was
the only information available to him.

The Remorse of David (1:17-27)

Rather than rejoicing in the death of his adversary,
David manifested the greatness of his heart as he
chanted a dirge (KJV, *"lamented with this lamentation"*) over
the fallen warriors (1:17). The title is given as "The
Bow" and was preserved in the *Book of Jasher* (1:18). The
Book of Jasher (literally, "the book of the righteous")
appears to have been a collection of songs related to
historical events which was used in an instructional
and inspirational manner. One other definite reference
to this book is found in the Hebrew Old Testament.
(See Joshua 10:12-14.)

The song contains three movements marked by the
phrase, *"How are the mighty fallen!" (1:19, 25, 27).* How
amazing that the poem contains no negative statements regarding Saul, no innuendos, no ugly vindictive
remarks! David was both eloquent and sincere in his
grief over Saul and Jonathan. What an example for us
who are tempted to weep over those who rejoice and to
rejoice over those who weep!

In the first section (1:19-24) both Saul and Jonathan
are eulogized, with primary emphasis on Saul. After a
declaration of Saul's death (he is referred to as the
"beauty" or "glory" of Israel—1:19), the poet pleaded
that the news not be published in Gath or Askelon (two
major Philistine cities) so that the enemy might not

rejoice over the fallen heroes (1:20). As if the mourning
of humanity were not enough, David invited nature to
join in the sorrow by withholding the dew, the rain,
and the fruit for offerings upon the mountains of Gilboa (1:21). In her fields the shield of the mighty warriors had been cast down in a dishonorable fashion. No
longer would Saul's shield be polished with its preserv-
ing oil, ready for battle. Now it was a blood-stained
memento of a slain king. But not all is negative. David
remembered the gallantry, goodness, and grandeur of
these men. Their gallantry had been demonstrated on
the field of battle (1:22). Their goodness is expressed in
the statement, *"Saul and Jonathan were lovely and pleasant in
their lives" (1:23)*. The word *"lovely"* means "beloved," and
"pleasant" means "good, delightful, sweet." Those are
amazing attributes for a man like Saul. Then the grandeur of the kingdom of Saul is alluded to in verse twenty-
four. Saul had provided his people with beautiful cloth-
ing, with luxuriant finery (KJV, *"delights"*), and with
ornaments of gold.

The second section focuses on Jonathan (1:25-26).
David's emotional distress was heightened by the loss
of his friend. Jonathan had been "good" for David (KJV,
"very pleasant"), had offered his counsel, his encouragement, and himself to David during David's most frus-
trating experiences. The relationship between these
two had been so strong that it is stated, *"Thy love to me
was wonderful, passing the love of women" (1:26)*. The Hebrew
word for *"wonderful"* implied an experience which was
beyond human capabilities. Often it is used in conjunc-
tion with the miracles of God. Capturing the sense of
this word, we might even say that the love between
these men was almost "unbelievable" or "incredible." In
fact, this love was stronger than the love of a man for a
woman.

The eulogy concludes, *"How are the mighty fallen, and the weapons of war perished!" (1:27)*. The reference to weapons of war is a veiled symbolism to Saul and Jonathan. With a sense of great loss, the dirge ends.

Only a man who walks closely with God, a man after God's own heart, could speak so mercifully and kindly about another who had wronged him. Why not expose Saul? Why not use Saul's death as a platform for self-promotion? David must have caught the spirit of what would be written over a millennium later, *"Brethren, if a man be overtaken in a fault, ye which are spiritual, restore such an one in the spirit of meekness; considering thyself, lest thou also be tempted" (Galatians 6:1)*.

TIMELESS TRUTHS FOR TODAY

---

1. Our reaction to the failures of others reveals the depth of our relationship with God.

2. When our enemies fall, we should restore and strengthen them, considering our own weaknesses.

Chapter 2

What Now, Lord?

II Samuel 2:1-32

Walt Disney has produced some delightful adaptations of A. A. Milne's classics about Christopher Robin and his friends who lived in the Hundred Acre Wood. One of my favorites is the story of the Blustery Day. Pooh and Piglet were visiting with Owl, when suddenly Owl's tree house was blown over and completely destroyed. Such a disaster brought all of the characters together to encourage Owl. The situation appeared beyond hope. A gross understatement was made by Eeyore, who declared, "If you ask me, when a house looks like that, it's time to move."

David's circumstances were not a lot better. His own home, along with those of all his followers, had been destroyed with fire by the Amalekites (I Samuel 30:1). Although David was able to recover the captives and goods, it would take time to reconstruct the city of Ziklag. For two days they cleared away the ashes and debris. Someone must have thought, "If you ask me, when a city looks like this, it's time to move." When word came of Saul's death, it would have been a temptation for David and his people to march into Israel and take over. But David had tasted the bitter fruit of hasty, selfish decisions. Now he demonstrated a complete surrender to God's ways and God's timing.

A Coronation at Hebron (2:1-7)

After the initial shock of Saul's death had worn off, David *enquired of the Lord,* using the Urim and Thummim (2:1; cf. I Samuel 23:4, 9; 30:7-8). Two questions are asked—When? and Where? First, he inquired, *"Shall I go up into any of the cities of Judah?"* Notice that David did not presume upon God. He sought guidance for this first step. That he should restrict his request to the cities of Judah shows both wisdom and humility. The cities of Israel, for the most part, had come under the domination of the Philistines. Therefore, they were unavailable. Besides, Saul had turned the hearts of the people against David. Nor were they even aware that David had been anointed by Samuel to be their king (I Samuel 16:1, 13). David knew that he would have to prove himself and win their loyalty. Though he would have to wait for a united kingdom, God directed David to return to his homeland.

"Whither shall I go up?" asked the cautious young man. His attitude was, "Lord, anywhere You want to send me is fine!" And God sent him to Hebron. The city of Hebron is the site of several important references in Scripture. When Abram was promised the land of Canaan, he moved there and built an altar unto the Lord (Genesis 13:14-18). It was from this place that the spies from the Israelite camp returned with a huge

cluster of grapes (Numbers 13:22-24). Later, Caleb
asked Joshua for this land, although it was inhabited by
giants and would be difficult to conquer (Joshua 14:6-
15). Hebron was also appointed as one of the cities of
refuge in the land of Israel (Joshua 20:1-7). From these
passages we see that Hebron signified four spiritual
truths.

With Abram, Hebron was a place of fellowship with
God and fulfillment of the promise. For the spies, it
represented a place of fruitfulness. Caleb's actions
spoke of Hebron as the place for the working of faith.
That this city was a place of refuge typifies the provision for forgiveness. Certainly, David must have recalled these events at Hebron and encouraged himself
in the grace of God that would allow him to go from
Ziklag (a place of desolation) to Hebron (a place of
blessing).

Having gathered his own family and those who followed him, David led the people more than twenty
miles to their new home (2:2-3). He was well received
and was soon anointed to be king over the house of
Judah (2:4). This was the second of David's three
anointings (I Samuel 16:13; II Samuel 5:3).

One of David's first acts as king was to send a message to the men of Jabesh-gilead (2:5). The inhabitants
of Judah had informed him of how these men had risked
their lives in honor of the former king (2:4). David's
correspondence was one of praise, prayer, promise, and
seeming proposition. He praised them for their kindness and valiance and promised that he would reward
them for their deeds (2:5-6). He also prayed that God
would grace them with kindness and truth as well (2:6).
His note concluded with a statement of his own recent
anointing as king of Judah (2:7). This seems to be a gen-
tle proposal to join the bandwagon. The message of

David was sincere, but it also showed his political savvy. If the men of Jabesh-gilead would join him, the new king would have made an important step in uniting the kingdom.

A Competitor at Mahanaim (2:8-11)

Abner, the captain of Saul's army, had somehow managed to escape death at the battle of Mount Gilboa. Possibly three to five years after David's ascension to the throne at Hebron, Abner appeared on the scene with a puppet king for the northern tribes. Ishbosheth, another of Saul's sons, had survived the Philistine assault. Perhaps he had not even participated in the battle. His name means "man of shame." He is also called Esh-baal, "man of baal" (I Chronicles 8:33). Does this imply that he followed false gods or was a disgrace to the family? We cannot be sure, but Old Testament names were used to reveal the character of the person. However, from the accounts of Ishbosheth in II Samuel, we learn that he was a weak man and a helpless pawn in Abner's hand.

With the passing of time, Abner had regrouped and recaptured some of the conquered northern cities. These he united and placed under the hand of Ishbosheth, who was now forty years old (2:10). The capital was established in Mahanaim, a major city on the east side of the Jordan. The eastern tribes had been loyal to Saul. Also, Mahanaim would be much safer from Philistine invasion.

A Confrontation at Gibeon (2:12-32)

Approximately six miles north of Jerusalem stood the town of Gibeon. It was the home of a shrewd and mighty people (Joshua 9:3-15; 10:2). The tabernacle had also been erected there after the slaughter of the priests by Saul and the destruction of Nob. (Cf. I Samuel 22:6-19; II Chronicles 1:3.) Gibeon was a strong city because of an abundant water supply. Even today the pool of Gibeon with its shaft (thirty-seven feet wide and thirty-five feet deep) can be viewed.

One day Abner from Israel and Joab from Judah left their respective cities on what might have been reconnaissance missions. Surprisingly, the two commanders and their armies met face-to-face at the pool of Gibeon (2:12-13). No immediate fighting took place, but the tension must have been great. Abner could finally restrain himself no longer. He issued a challenge that the champions of each army meet in a contest (2:14). This type of warfare was not unusual in the ancient world (I Samuel 17:4-10). Twelve soldiers were chosen from each side, but within moments all twenty-four lay dead (2:15-16). In this particular contest the men had paired off and were allowed to take hold of each other's hair in order to keep them in close proximity. Since the word for "sword" in Hebrew could also mean dagger (as in the Greek Septuagint), it seems that this was not a sword fight but a hand-to-hand combat.

Of course, there was no victor since all were killed. As a result, intense fighting broke out (2:17). Abner and his men were beaten and scattered. Under the leadership of Zeruiah's three sons—Joab, Abishai, and Asahel—David's troops pursued the northern armies. Asahel, who could run like a gazelle, followed after Abner with unwavering determination (2:19). Abner recognized his pursuer and repeatedly urged him to "give up" the chase (2:20-21). Abner further warned Asahel that he would kill him if necessary (2:22). But the young commander would not be deterred from his goal (2:23). With no apparent alternatives, Abner thrust the opposite end of his spear into the onrushing Asahel. The spear impaled the son of Zeruiah and he died. Those who followed Asahel stopped when they came to their dead leader (2:23).

Joab and Abishai continued the hunt until evening to the hill of Ammah near Giah (exact site unknown). There Abner regrouped his men and issued a call for peace (2:26). Abner realized he could not win and that any further fighting would be bitter. Joab then reminded Abner that none of the bloodshed would have taken place if Abner had not demanded a confrontation (2:14, 27). Nevertheless, Joab sounded retreat with the ram's horn, the shofar (2:28).

Wearily, Abner and his men walked all night through the Jordan Valley and by midday reached the capital of Mahanaim (2:29). Joab meanwhile took his dead brother to Bethlehem to be buried and then marched all night, reaching Hebron at daybreak (2:32). The final toll of the losses was 20 dead of David's men and 360 dead of Abner's soldiers (2:30-31).

Surrender to the will of God does not automatically guarantee that things will be easy. Although David now possessed a kingdom, it was a divided one. Frictions had already begun to surface. They usually do when one person wants to exalt the Lord and the other exalts self. But David was determined to do right, regardless of the opposition or the friction it created. Have you made that total surrender to the will of God? It will not be easy, but no one promised that it would be.

TIMELESS TRUTHS FOR TODAY

1. Surrender to God's will necessitates humility.
2. Surrender to God's will demands availability.
3. Surrender to God's will produces hostility.

Chapter **3**

Now Then Do It!
II Samuel 3:1-21

Human nature can be so predictable at times. Have you ever seen a sign that said, "Wet paint—do not touch!"? Now be honest; what did you do? I would like a nickel for every time that I've had to wash my hands after encountering that sign. There's just something in us that drives us to "do" when we are told, "Do not." That attitude crosses over into every area of our lives—including the decisions to do right or wrong. Paul had similar problems: *"For the good that I would I do not: but the evil which I would not, that I do. I find then a law, that, when I would do good, evil is present with me"* (Romans 7:19, 21). Have you ever felt like that? Surely you have. But what is it that creates those opposing desires? Paul revealed that there is a war going on between flesh and spirit: *"For the flesh lusteth against the Spirit, and the Spirit against the flesh: and these are contrary the one to the other: so that ye cannot do the things that ye would"* (Galatians 5:17).

This conflict is illustrated in the third chapter of II Samuel. The kingdom had become divided between the house of Saul and the house of David (2:8-11). As a result, there was a continuous state of hostility between the two. (Note the references to *"long war"* and *"war"* in 3:1, 6). Nevertheless, we read, *"But David waxed stronger and stronger, and the house of Saul waxed weaker and weaker" (3:1).* The house of Saul, symbolic of the works of the flesh, had been made low. Quickly they were coming to the end of their rope. But David, symbolic of life in the Spirit, was gaining strength by the minute, which reminds us of another statement by Paul: *"For which cause we faint not."* For what *"cause"*? He did not faint in spite of the trouble, distress, perplexities, and persecutions that he endured (II Corinthians 4:16). Are you struggling to live a victorious Christian life? Let's examine the story and observe some key problems and necessary solutions for victorious living.

The Posterity of David (3:1-5)

In order to verify the increasing strength of David's house, the writer of II Samuel has included a list of David's sons born at Hebron. Of the six sons, three later gained notoriety. Amnon committed incest with his brother's sister (13:1-17). Absalom rebelled against his father (14—17). Adonijah tried to wrest the throne from his brother Solomon (I Kings 1:5). The other three—Chileab, Shephatiah, and Ithream—have remained in relative obscurity.

All six sons were born of different women. David had come to Hebron with only two wives, Ahinoam and Abigail (2:2). Maacah, Haggith, Abital, and Eglah were acquired while in Hebron. Maacah is called *"the daughter of Talmai king of Geshur" (3:3).* Living within the

inheritance of Israel were the Geshurites, an uncon-
quered people (Joshua 13:11, 13). The territory was
located east of the Jordan and Sea of Galilee in the
general vicinity of what we call the Golan Heights today. The marriage between David and Maacah revealed
political overtones. David felt that a political alliance
through marriage would insure some stability in the
northeastern part of the kingdom. It also provided him
with an ally to the north of Ishbosheth's domain. But
we should also point out that Maacah was a "foreign"
wife. Perhaps this helped produce Absalom's indepen-
dent spirit.

A Problem Between Abner and Ishbosheth (3:6-11)

Although David's power and influence were growing
and the house of Saul was diminishing, one man in the
North was making a concerted effort to retain control.
That man was Abner (3:6). Ishbosheth was not blind to
Abner's actions. Finally, after Abner had cohabited
with one of Saul's concubines, Rizpah, Ishbosheth confronted him (3:7).

Before we go further, we must answer two questions: What is a concubine, and why were Abner's actions so serious? First, a concubine represented a form
of polygamy. Usually, it was reserved for kings or men
of great wealth. The concubine was a wife who only
enjoyed a secondary status to the primary wife or
wives. She could be easily divorced, and her children
could be excluded from the father's inheritance by
means of a simple gift.

Ishbosheth's strong reaction to Abner's relationship
to Rizpah is understandable when we realize that a
former king's concubines became the "property" of the
new king. For a man to have sexual relations with a

king's concubine was equivalent to usurping the right
of the throne. (For illustrations, see II Samuel 12:8;
16:21-22; I Kings 2:21-22.) Ishbosheth rightly inter-
preted Abner's deed as an attempt to "strengthen himself" in power.

Faced with the question, Abner responded in anger.
The literal Hebrew states that he was "burning" because of the rebuke. Rather than answering Ishbosheth,
he unleashed an emotional tirade: "Am I a dog's head
which belongs to Judah?" A dog in oriental culture was
a lowly beast, a contemptible animal. Abner wondered
if he were being accused as a traitor (i.e., loyal to Judah).
He appealed to his past kindness to Saul's house and his
present protection of Ishbosheth as proof of his loyalty.
"How can you charge me with such a fault?" The word
for *"fault"* in verse eight means to bend, twist, distort,
pervert. It is often translated as *"iniquity"* in our Bibles.
Contained in the meaning is not only the idea of sin but
also the accompanying guilt. Even though Abner was
upset at the charges, he never denied them. His reaction out of guilt seemed to validate the charge. This
brings us to the question, "How do you react to rebuke?" Solomon wrote, *"Reprove not a scorner, lest he hate
thee: rebuke a wise man, and he will love thee" (Proverbs 9:8).*
Obviously, Abner was a scorner and hated Ishbosheth
for the rebuke. (For a contrast, see David's reaction to
Nathan's rebuke in II Samuel 12:1-13.) From that point
on, Abner was determined to transfer the kingdom of
Saul's house to David (3:9-10). Since Ishbosheth was a
puppet ruler and feared Abner, he could do nothing to
stop this plan (3:11).

When Abner was confronted with his sin, what
should he have done? How could he have rid himself of
the accompanying guilt? In examining the passages
that contain the Hebrew word for *"fault,"* I discovered

four steps necessary to remove sin and its guilt.

STEP ONE: Recognize and confess sin (Genesis 44:16; Leviticus 16:21; Psalm 32:5; 38:18).

STEP TWO: Request pardon from God for sin (Exodus 34:9; Numbers 14:19; Psalm 25:11).

STEP THREE: Repent and turn from sin (Ezekiel 18:30-32).

STEP FOUR: Receive God's payment for sin (Leviticus 16:22; Isaiah 53:5-6).

By following these four steps, you, too, can be freed from the bondage and guilt of sin.

A Proposal from Abner to David (3:12-21)

Within a short time after the confrontation between Abner and Ishbosheth, messengers were on their way to Judah, offering to David a covenant between the two countries (3:12). The message read, *"Whose is the land?"* The answer was apparent that it belonged to David. The message continued, *"Make thy league with me, and, behold, my hand shall be with thee, to bring about all Israel unto thee" (3:12).*

The reply came back, "Good!" (3:13). This was the best news that David had heard in years. He was willing to make such a covenant, with one requirement. Michal, Saul's daughter, would first have to be returned to David. David had married Michal after providing an unusual dowry (I Samuel 18:20-27). Michal had loved David very much and had protected him from her father's wrath (I Samuel 18:20, 28; 19:11-17). But when David became a fugitive in the desert, Saul gave Michal to a man from Gallim named Phalti (I Samuel 25:44). Now David wanted her because he wanted to be reunited with his wife and wanted to lay claims to the house of Saul, since she was Saul's daughter.

Word of the request came to Ishbosheth, who sent for her through Abner (3:14-15). Phaltiel, her second husband, followed her a short distance from Gallim to Bahurim, weeping loudly all the way. Being fed up with the distraction, Abner ordered Phaltiel to return home (3:16). Michal was then delivered to David.

In the meantime, Abner had communicated with the leaders of Israel. In time past they had been disenchanted with Saul; and later, with Ishbosheth. In this disenchantment they had desired to anoint David as their king (3:17). Abner reiterated to them the word of the Lord concerning David—that he would bring deliverance to Israel (3:18). To guarantee full support for his effort, Abner met individually with the Benjamites, Saul's tribe, and convinced them of the need to follow David (3:19). Essentially, Abner's appeal was, *"Ye sought for David in times past to be king over you; Now then do it" (3:17-18)*. They knew the right thing to do. All that was left was the doing of it.

With the elders of Israel united in their desire for David, Abner took twenty men and went to Hebron 3:20). A feast was prepared and the two men talked over plans for uniting the kingdom (3:21). After the details had been finalized, Abner and his men departed in peace from Hebron.

We began by saying that the struggle between Ishbosheth ("man of shame") and David ("beloved") was symbolic of the conflict between the flesh and the spirit. Early in the chapter Abner's actions were a manifestation of life in the flesh. He sought strength in himself (3:6), fulfilled his own fleshly desires (3:7), demonstrated pride by not admitting his sin (3:8), displayed an uncontrolled temperament (3:8), and acted according to wrong motivation (3:9). Yet the passage ends in *"peace"* *(3:21)*. How is this possible? Peace was brought about by three things. First, there was the claiming of God's promise. Abner knew that David was the rightful heir to the throne (3:12). God had promised it (3:18). Next, there was the surrendering of the will. Abner met with the leaders of Israel to convince them of what was right and that they would have to submit to David (3:17-19). Finally, there was the purposing to do right. *"Now then do it"* (3:18). So often we know God's principles and are convinced of their truthfulness, but the problem develops when we fail to follow through in doing right. Let's face it—most of us know what is right. What we need is the character to *"do it."*

TIMELESS TRUTHS FOR TODAY

For peace to reign in my heart:

1. **God's Word must be supreme.**

2. **My will must be surrendered.**

3. **My ways must be steadfast.**

Chapter 4

The Game of Life

II Samuel 3:22-39

There is a popular board game on the market under the name **The Game of Life**. The game begins by moving through a series of educational squares to decide a player's salary structure. Continuing through the maze, a wife and children are added, and the normal difficulties of life are encountered. Spaces marked REVENGE are the game's most popular feature. When landing on one of those spots, the player is entitled to penalize an opposing player. (Most games are built on this principle of revenge.) The player seeking revenge hopes to get ahead through the calamity of another. In playing this game, I have always noticed the devious look of a player who lands on "revenge," not to mention my own sinister feelings. There are shouts of joy and moans of despair. But the problem is that as you take revenge on someone, he will try to get even with you. That's **The Game of Life.**

Unfortunately, Milton Bradley does not have a corner on the market. Most people play the real game of life the same way. Given the chance, people will often take advantage of others in order to promote themselves. I like the words of one wise sage who said, "You can never get ahead of anyone so long as you are trying to get even with him."

Paul's words to the Romans are in direct opposition to the world's philosophy of life. *"Recompense to no man evil for evil . . . If it be possible, as much as lieth in you, live peaceably with all men. Dearly beloved, avenge not yourselves, but rather give place unto wrath: for it is written, Vengeance is mine; I will repay, saith the Lord. Therefore if thine enemy hunger, feed him; if he thirst, give him drink: for in so doing thou shalt heap coals of fire on his head. Be not overcome of evil, but overcome evil with good"* (Romans 12:17-21). Had Joab, one of David's captains, lived by that principle, he would have been spared from living with a terrible memory.

The Suspicion of Joab (3:22-25)

Previously in chapter three Abner, the captain of the northern armies, had offered to make a league with David (3:12). Abner had come to Hebron with twenty men to discuss the matter with the southern king (3:20). Having laid all the plans for uniting the divided country, Abner retraced his steps to Mahanaim (3:21).

Soon after Abner's departure, Joab returned to the city of Hebron with the spoil he had acquired during a raid upon the enemies (3:22). A group of skeptics who had questioned David's entertaining of the northern commander approached Joab and told him of the recent events (3:23). Joab was incensed to think that Abner had been permitted to come and go in peace. Immediately, he voiced his suspicions to the king (3:24-25).

First, he rebuked David for letting a "golden opportunity" slip by. "What have you done?" Joab questioned. "You had Abner in the palm of your hand, and you let him get away. Not only that—you sent him away in peace." The underlying sentiment was that David should have killed Abner and taken Israel by force while he had a chance.

Joab proceeded to question Abner's motives. *"Thou knowest Abner the son of Ner, that he came to deceive thee" (3:25).* *"Deceive"* is an interesting word in the Hebrew language. The basic meaning—"to be open, spacious, wide"— refers more to the one being deceived than of the act itself. What Joab really said was, "David, how could you be so simple, so naive, as to believe that Abner came here with pure motives? He has persuaded you to think that he is your friend." Joab believed that Abner had come to determine how David operated and thus lay the groundwork for a surprise attack against Hebron (3:25).

The Slaying of Abner (3:26-27, 30)

King David must have been unimpressed and unconvinced by his captain, for he took no precautions. Seeing the futility of further argument, Joab decided to take matters into his own hands. Besides, he felt that he had an account that had to be settled.

After leaving the presence of David, Joab sent a messenger to catch Abner (3:26). Abner had not traveled far since the Scripture records that he returned to Hebron from the well of Sirah. (This well is identified with the well of Sarah, approximately one mile north of Hebron.) Joab met Abner at the gate of the city and must have feigned friendship. Privately, Joab took his victim to the middle of the gate to perform

his treachery. The gate of Hebron, like most gates of
Old Testament cities, was likely composed of a covered
corridor with several chambers for guards on either
side. Joab probably led Abner into this corridor where it
would be darker and then backed him into one of the
chambers under the pretense of seeking privacy. There
Joab struck the unsuspecting leader in the belly with
his knife. Only then is the true motive for the murder
revealed: *"He died, for the blood of Asahel his* [Joab's] *brother"*
(3:27). This reason is reinforced in verse thirty, where
we learn that Abishai, another brother, was also involved in the wicked plot.

Although Abner may not have been an angel, he certainly did not deserve to die in revenge of Asahel. Asahel's death was in self-defense and after repeated warnings of dire consequences. (See II Samuel 2:19-23.) David
also agreed that Abner should not have died as he did
(3:33-34). The seriousness of this brutal act was com-
pounded by the fact that Joab had avenged his brother's
blood in a city of refuge (Joshua 20:1-7).

The Sorrow of David (3:28-39)

Swiftly, news of the event reached David, who publicly declared his own innocence in the matter (3:28).
The king knew that such a death would be a blot to his
kingdom. In the interest of justice David said, *"Let it* [the
guilt] *rest on the head of Joab, and on all his father's house"*
(3:29). Accompanying this curse were five provisions.
Everyone of the house of Joab would suffer from one of
these five conditions. The first two spoke of diseases
(*"one that hath an issue, or that is a leper"*). (See also Leviticus
15; 22:4; Numbers 5:2.) The third provision was one of
physical weakness (*"one . . . that leaneth on a staff"*). Some
believe that this may refer to effeminate characteristics

when compared to the staff (or distaff) of Proverbs 31:19. The fourth curse asked for tragic death (*"or that falleth on the sword"*), while the concluding one brought about poverty (*"or that lacketh bread"*).

In order to prove further his innocence and exonerate his kingdom, David ordered that there should be public mourning. *"Rend your clothes, and gird you with sackcloth, and mourn before Abner"* (3:31). David himself followed the bier to the grave. At the burial the king was the first to be heard weeping (3:32). Composing himself, David eulogized the fallen warrior. *"Died Abner as a fool dieth? Thy hands were not bound, nor thy feet put into fetters: as a man falleth before wicked men, so fellest thou"* (3:33-34).

David's lament reveals two important facts. The death of Abner was carried out in a cruel, merciless fashion. How impressive that the king did not try to hide the truth! As Solomon wrote, *"He that covereth his sins shall not prosper: but whoso confesseth and forsaketh them shall have mercy"* (Proverbs 28:13). Also in David's eulogy is again the revealing of the culprits. They are labeled as *"wicked men"* (literally, "sons of evil"). Abner certainly deserved better than to fall at the hands of such men. The words struck a responsive chord in the hearts of the people, for they wept even more over the death (3:34).

The burial must have been early in the day because David is later offered food while it is still day (3:35). But David had committed himself to a fast for the rest of the day; therefore, he would take no food (3:35). The people took careful note of these reactions by the king; they were pleased, and they respected the king for it (3:36). Only a man with a clear conscience could have done what David did. David's innocence was accepted (3:37).

Back at the king's residence, his servants were

gathered for a final testimonial. Joab and Abishai were certainly among them. David said, *"Know ye not that there is a prince and a great man fallen this day in Israel? And I am this day weak, though anointed king; and these men the sons of Zeruiah be too hard for me: the Lord shall reward the doer of evil according to his wickedness" (3:38-39).* Several things are significant about this statement. First, David recognized the greatness and uniqueness of each of his subjects. Second, he realized that his kingdom would be only as strong as his weakest servant. Third, he revealed that any wrongdoing would be identified and punished by the Lord. No wonder David's kingdom prospered.

Joab's actions cost him dearly. In avenging his brother's blood, he lost three things. He lost a clear conscience because he murdered an "innocent" man in a city of refuge. He lost the commendation of the king. In verse thirty-nine he and his brother are said to be *"too hard"* (or a burden) for David. And Joab lost the confidence that his family would be prosperous for future generations. Revenge is an expensive proposition in the game of life—for everyone involved. Therefore, maybe our motto should be, "I will try to get even only with those who have helped me in some way."

TIMELESS TRUTHS FOR TODAY

---

1. Nothing can replace the peace of a clear conscience.

2. Nothing can replace the joy of a good testimony.

3. Nothing can replace the hope of a strong family.

Chapter 5

Little Things Are Important
II Samuel 4:1-12

Several years ago when we first moved to Denver, my wife and I invited some friends over to our new home for fellowship and dessert. Since homemade ice cream pleases almost everyone, that was our choice for the refreshments. As is usually the case, time got away and we were hurriedly trying to complete our preparations before the guests arrived. I was just dumping the ice in the ice cream freezer as our friends rang the doorbell. Whew! We just made it! Relaxing on that pleasant Colorado evening, everything seemed to be going well.

As we talked with the other couples, I could hardly wait for that ice cream to freeze. Eventually, it was time to check on the dessert. Opening the top revealed the creamy treat—ready to be devoured. After serving our guests, we sat down to enjoy ourselves. But with the first bite, everyone knew that something was wrong. An uneasiness sets in, and people feel awkward in such situations. The ice cream did not taste bad; it just didn't taste! What was wrong? In an instant my wife realized that in the last-minute rush she had forgotten to add the vanilla. Although we were embarrassed, all was not lost. After we had discovered the problem, we laughed—and the ice cream seemed to taste better.

Forgetting a "little thing" like adding the vanilla to vanilla ice cream is not a catastrophic event, even though it made a difference in the taste. But there are many "things" which are critical to life which some people consider "little." God's Word consistently warns us about the importance of small things. One post-exilic prophet wrote, *"Who hath despised the day of small things?" (Zechariah 4:10)*. The temple of Zerubbabel had a foundation much smaller than the glorious temple of Solomon. This had caused some people to lose heart. Zechariah was writing to encourage them not to look at the **size** of the temple but at the **significance** of that house.

How many people do you know who are looking for "larger" opportunities rather than faithfully fulfilling "smaller" responsibilities? The criterion for greater opportunity is being reliable in handling "little things." Christ Himself said, *"He that is faithful in that which is least is faithful also in much" (Luke 16:10)*.

On the surface the story found in II Samuel 4 may seem totally unrelated to what we have just said. Ishbosheth appears to be the central figure. He is brutally slain, and the northern kingdom comes to an end. However, we should not miss the lesson taught by an unlikely quartet—a nurse, a doorkeeper, and two captains. They all became careless in little things, and it cost them in a big way.

The Confusion in the Kingdom (4:1-3)

Possibly from the twenty men who had accompanied Abner to Hebron (3:20), King Ishbosheth learned of the death of his military commander. Upon hearing the report, it is stated that *"his hands were feeble" (4:1)*. Although the word *"feeble"* often conveys the idea of loss of ability due to old age, here the meaning is that Ishbosheth became disheartened. Literally, the word means to "sink down or let drop." It is as if Ishbosheth had stretched out his fist as a symbol of power, but with Abner gone his hand dropped to his side in despair. Ishbosheth knew that his days were numbered.

The king was not the only person in the kingdom who was disturbed over Abner's death. *"All the Israelites were troubled" (4:1)*. Another way of translating that phrase would be, "All the Israelites were terrified." Inherent in this expression is the emotional response that is generated when someone is confronted by an unexpected, potentially disastrous situation. An illustration of this terror is recorded in the Book of Judges. A Levite, his concubine, and a servant were returning to his home in the land of Ephraim when he stopped for the evening in the Benjamite town of Gibeah. During the night wicked men surrounded the home and demanded that the Levite commit sodomy with them (Judges 19:22). The host refused to permit such a vile act. Instead, the concubine was given to the men, who abused her throughout the night. By the next morning she was dead. The leaders of Benjamin refused to bring justice upon the men who had done this wickedness (Judges 20:13). Therefore, in retaliation, the other tribes of Israel decided to fight against Benjamin. The third attack proved successful when the Israelites surrounded the wayward tribe, leaving no way of escape. It was then that the Benjamites saw their predicament

and became terrified (KJV—*"amazed"* in Judges 20:41).
The same feeling of hopelessness and helplessness now
cast its shadow on the entire northern kingdom.

Adding to the confusion was a leaderless army that
was composed of many mercenaries who had attained
positions of leadership. Two of these captains, Baanah
and Rechab, were Beerothites. Beeroth, a small town
approximately nine miles north of Jerusalem, had
originally been allied with Gibeon in an act of deception
against the Israelites (Joshua 9:1-19). During Saul's
reign a persecution had arisen against the Gibeonites
(II Samuel 21:1). If this oppression included the men of
Beeroth, it might explain the flight from Beeroth to
Gittaim as well as the actions of Baanah and Rechab
against the house of Saul (II Samuel 4:3).

The Carelessness of Two Servants (4:4-6)

The incident involving Mephibosheth seems out of
place at this point in the narrative (4:4). The episode
related is a flashback to the events surrounding I
Samuel 31. When it was known that Saul and three of
his sons had died, Saul's capital at Gibeah suffered
pandemonium. The city was evacuated. While trying to
escape impending disaster, a nurse (or guardian) picked
up the five-year-old Mephibosheth and ran for safety.
The word for *"nurse"* in the Hebrew means "one who
supports, upholds, is faithful." This nurse was careless
and dropped the lad, and he was lame the rest of his
life. She did not conscientiously keep her charge. Failure followed, and its effects were permanent.

Why the reference to Mephibosheth? After Ishbosheth, he would normally be considered heir apparent
to the throne. However, his physical disability disquali-
fied him from becoming king. Near-eastern custom

dictates that no "flawed" individual could be king. Mephibosheth's injury not only opened the door to a Davidic dynasty but also created further confusion to the northern tribes concerning future successors.

Before we consider the conspiracy of the two captains, we ought to observe the carelessness of another individual. He is unnamed in Scripture. In fact, there is not a word spoken about him. As you read verses five and six, a missing detail becomes conspicuous. Rechab and Baanah entered Ishbosheth's room by pretending to be refurbishing their supplies (4:6). Why did they have to pretend to be someone they were not? Because a doorkeeper stood by the door to guard the life of the king. This man, like the nurse, was careless in "little things." Maybe he thought that his position was unimportant, but it was not. His failure cost the king his life, and it cost him his job.

The Conspiracy of Two Captains (4:5-8)

Baanah and Rechab seized the opportunity of self-promotion. These men were mercenary soldiers from Beeroth who led two bands of marauders (4:2). By the standards of most people, these soldiers were outlaws. (Someone had been careless in choosing the right kind of leadership.) Their plan to assassinate the king worked perfectly. The story reads like the plot of a modern novel.

In the heat of the day they approached the king's quarters (4:5). Knowing that the king took his nap during that period, they could successfully carry out their plan. Activities would be minimal, and the presence of servants would be scarce. All that they needed to do was get past the doorkeeper. Since the king usually stored provisions for his soldiers in his own house, the two captains pretended to be getting supplies for their men (4:6). Not questioning their authority, the guard admitted them. Within moments Rechab and Baanah stabbed and beheaded Ishbosheth (4:6-7). As they exited past the guard, they were carrying a sack of what appeared to be wheat—but inside was the head of the king.

Immediately leaving Mahanaim, the men journeyed all night through the Jordan Valley and across the fords of the Jordan (4:7). This gave them a good start against any pursuing troop. Finally they arrived in Hebron and presented David with the evidence of Ishbosheth's death, saying, *"Behold the head of Ishbosheth the son of Saul thine enemy, which sought thy life; and the Lord hath avenged my lord the king this day of Saul, and of his seed"* (4:8). By that statement they tried to justify and even lend an air of spirituality to their deed.

The Condemnation from David (4:9-12)

It would seem that David's integrity would be known by now. The righteous king of Judah would not be a party to treachery. In condemning Rechab and Baanah, David manifested several sterling qualities. First, we see his dependency upon God. He did not need to resort to fleshly means to overcome his adversity. He trusted in the Lord: *"As the Lord liveth, who hath redeemed my soul out of all adversity"* (4:9). Second, we see his integrity of heart. He related how he had slain the man who confessed to the murder of Saul (4:10). Saul's supposed executioner, like these two captains, thought to receive promotion by compromising convictions. In essence the king was saying, "The end does not justify the means." Third, we see his consistency of life. David reasoned that if he had killed Saul's murderer, how could he spare them (4:11). Especially is this true since David considered Ishbosheth as a righteous man (4:11). Godly dependency, genuine integrity, and personal consistency—these were the characteristics of the man after God's own heart!

Rechab and Baanah were executed and had their hands and feet cut off. Then they were publicly hanged by the pool of Hebron as a warning to all who would attempt such crimes (4:12). Ishbosheth was honored by a decent burial alongside Abner in Hebron.

The death of Ishbosheth is the central story, but the supporting cast teach us the important lesson of being faithful in "little things." The nurse at Gibeah was not faithful in her duties. The doorkeeper at Mahanaim was not faithful in his defense of the king. The two captains from Beeroth were not faithful in their devotion to their leader.

We all have been guilty of letting "little things" slip by. Sometimes it is the "little things" involved in duties. At other times it is carelessness in defending ourselves against the little enemies that try to sneak into our inner lives—wrong attitudes, wrong philosophies, wrong actions. Just as deadly are the "little things" that quench our devotion for the Lord. Be careful about the "little things" in life; they make the difference between success and failure.

TIMELESS TRUTHS FOR TODAY

1. It is not the "size" of the job that is important, but the "significance."

2. It is not the "big things" in life that will defeat and discourage you, but the "little things."

Chapter 6

A New Capital
for a New King
II Samuel 5:1-25

"And they lived happily ever after!"

No doubt a statement like that creates visions of boy meets girl, dreams come true, and fantasies become realities. That's the stuff fairy tales are made of.

David's accession as king over all Israel has all the earmarks of a dream come true. All of his hopes and aspirations find fulfillment in the early verses of II Samuel 5. However, the chapter does not end, "And he lived happily ever after!" In fact, before the king can even warm the seat of his new throne, he is embroiled in three strategic battles. Now, that's what real life is all about . . . especially the Christian life. When you crown Christ King of your life, problems do not vanish; conflicts do not subside. Someone might try to convince you that life transforms into a rose garden, but never forget that the thorns are still there. As we look into the story of this chapter in David's life, we

45

will observe many parallels to the life of a Christian who has made a complete surrender to the ways of God.

The Crowning of the King (5:1-5)

Ishbosheth was dead. The people of the northern tribes had nowhere to turn except to the southern monarch, who had consistently been gracious to the northern tribes and its leaders. Assembling a large delegation of over 340,000 men, Israel humbly came to David to crown him as their king (cf. I Chronicles 12:23-40). Three reasons are given as to why David should be their ruler. First, David was one of their own: *"Behold, we are thy bone and thy flesh" (5:1).* This is in harmony with the prerequisites for a king found in the Law of Moses (Deuteronomy 17:15). A second reason for choosing David is that he had been a leader of the people under Saul's administration (5:2). Specifically, he had been a victorious commander of the armies (I Samuel 18:5). The third reason was the most important. God had established David to be king: *"And the Lord said to thee, Thou shalt feed my people Israel, and thou shalt be a captain over Israel" (5:2).* The word *"feed"* is the same word used of David's keeping the sheep in I Samuel 16:11. David was still to be a shepherd—nourishing, protecting, leading. He simply changed flocks.

Discussion concerning the nature of the kingdom certainly followed, for King David made a covenant (*"league"*) with them. This covenant enumerated the conditions to be accepted by Israel if David was to be ruler. Upon coming to terms, David was anointed by the elders in Hebron (5:3). Two other anointings had preceded this event (I Samuel 16:13; II Samuel 2:4).

A celebration ensued that rivaled any in history.

Possibly 400,000 participated in a three-day feast that had been prepared in Hebron (I Chronicles 12:39). Some of the northern tribes had also brought numerous provisions for the banquet (I Chronicles 12:40). The people were as one (I Chronicles 12:38). A new dynasty had been set up. There was *"joy in Israel" (I Chronicles 12:40).*

The writer of II Samuel adds a note about the reign of David in verses four and five. At thirty years of age the shepherd had begun to rule in Hebron. For seven and one-half years he had led the people of Judah. Now he would move to a new capital, to shepherd God's people for another thirty-three years, making the total length of his reign over forty years.

The Capture of Jerusalem (5:6-16)

It was apparent that David could no longer stay in Hebron. Being a city in Judah, Hebron would cause his new subjects to question his loyalty to them. Since this city was also deep in the heart of Judah, it would not be easily accessible to the entire nation. A neutral site acceptable to both sides had to be sought.

For hundreds of years a stronghold of Canaanites had held their ground in a city in Israel. During the initial invasion of the land, Joshua and his men had been thwarted in all attempts to conquer these people (Joshua 15:63). The town was called Jebus, and its inhabitants the Jebusites. Since it was centrally located and also had been a nagging thorn in their side for generations, the capture of this town would prove to be a decided boost to David's image.

With all Israel following, David marched twenty miles to the seemingly impregnable fortress (I Chronicles 11:4). So confident were the Jebusites that they

boasted that even the blind and lame could defend their
city against this new threat (5:6). Carefully surveying
the area, David found their Achilles' heel. Near the
southern edge of the town outside the walls was an
underground spring named the Gihon. The Jebusites
had dug a shaft under their walls and down to this
spring to provide a safe water supply in case of a siege.
David challenged his men, *"Whosoever getteth up to the gutter,
and smiteth the Jebusites first shall be chief and captain"* (5:8 and
I Chronicles 11:6).

Perhaps because of his loss of status over Abner's
death (II Samuel 3:28, 29, 39), Joab took the initiative to
capture the city (I Chronicles 11:6). The attack came as
a complete surprise, and David's forces were victorious
(5:7). A program of refortification was begun in the city
immediately (5:9). David himself supervised the
strengthening of the Millo (either a fortress on the
northern plateau or a group of terraces on the eastern
side of the city) while Joab repaired the rest of the area
(I Chronicles 11:8). The new capital was called the city
of David (5:7). Today we know it as Jerusalem.

Recognition of the new government came quickly.
Hiram, King of Tyre, who was an enemy of the
Philistines, welcomed the new ally (5:11). He sent a
personal envoy along with cedar trees, carpenters, and
masons. As a gift, Hiram built a magnificent palace for
David. The new kingdom was going and growing
(5:10). What was David's secret? The Lord was with
him (5:10), and the people were unified in following
God's commands (5:12; cf. I Chronicles 12:32, 33, 38).

One blot spoils an otherwise perfect picture. When
David came to Jerusalem, he again took to himself more
concubines and wives (5:13). Very likely they were
Jebusites. The king allowed himself the unholy luxury
of following the pattern of the world's monarchs.

However, God had clearly stated concerning Israel's king, *"Neither shall he multiply wives to himself, that his heart turn not away" (Deuteronomy 17:17)*. (Although David did not appear to be affected by this disobedience, his son Solomon would practice the same sin and suffer greatly.) David's marriages produced more offspring in Jerusalem—including Solomon (5:14-16).

The Conquest of the Philistines (5:17-25)

So long as David was isolated in Judah, the Philistines had not considered him a serious enemy. But when it was learned that all Israel had united behind him, their opinion changed. Coming directly to the vicinity of Jerusalem from the southwest, the Philistines set up camp in the valley of Rephaim (5:18). *"Rephaim,"* meaning "giants," was a valley between Bethlehem and Jerusalem. David had begun his military career facing a Philistine giant in a valley (I Samuel 17). Now he must meet the Philistines again in the valley of the giants.

Though much older, he had not forgotten how to overcome the enemy. Seeking the guidance of his God, David prayed and was told to attack his oppressors (5:19). As was the case with Goliath, God went before him and fought the battle. The defeat scattered the opposition. They even left gods behind (5:21). In obedience to Old Testament law, David burned the idols (Deuteronomy 7:5). As a memorial of the victory, the site was called Baal-perazim, "master of the breakthroughs" (5:20). Men and women who crown Christ King of their lives often find themselves confronted with all-too-familiar enemies. It seems that the battles in the valley of the giants are always with us. Just when we think there can be no escape, no victory, we discover that God is still "Master of the breakthroughs."

A second encounter with the Philistines soon occurred. The attack was centered once more in the valley of Rephaim (5:22). However, when David inquired
of the Lord this time, he received different instructions
(5:23). His armies were to encircle (KJV, *"fetch a compass"*)
the enemy and wait behind a group of trees (baka trees,
similar to balsams). Then they were to listen for a
sound of marching in the treetops (5:24). The significance, of course, is that this was the sound of God's
armies marching before the men into battle. Once that
sound was heard, David was to *"bestir"* himself. Literally,
the word means "to cut, to be sharp," conveying the
idea of being alert and quick to action. David soundly
defeated and chased his enemy from the area of Jerusalem all the way to the coastal plains (5:25). The Book of
Chronicles adds, *"And the fame of David went out into all
lands; and the Lord brought the fear of him upon all nations"* (I
Chronicles 14:17).

The parallels between this chapter and the Christian
life are obvious. Israel is symbolic of the man or woman
who struggles with the Lordship of Christ. When
David (a type of Christ) was crowned, the real conflicts
began. Jerusalem typifies the "thorn" that may have
plagued us throughout our lives—an inward battle,
usually with self or some sinful habit. It is a stronghold
that must be conquered before there is power in the
life. Then comes the outward opposition by our
adversary. To walk into this "valley of the giants" can
be fearful indeed. Constant prayer and a vigilant watch
are our weapons. But God will always go before us to
help us fight the battles. And just as David enjoyed a
widespread fame as a result of his victories, so also will
the testimony of the Christian be evident to the world
when he or she conquers self, sin, and Satan.

While it is true that the Lord never promised us an easy road, we must not forget that He has promised to walk that road with us. One day, when we come to the end of that road, we will "live happily ever after!" That will be no fairy tale—it will be eternal life.

TIMELESS TRUTHS FOR TODAY

1. Making Christ King of your life means meeting Him on His terms, not yours.

2. Making Christ King of your life means conflict, not ease.

3. Making Christ King of your life means success, not failure.

4. Making Christ King of your life means life, not death.

Chapter 7

When All Else Fails— Read the Instructions
II Samuel 6:1-23

Recently I took my younger daughter out to eat at a fast-food restaurant. (They really know how to attract the kids with their colorful characters and unique playgrounds.) Of course, I ordered the special children's meal for her—you know, the one that has the toy inside. After the blessing, it was as if my little girl said, "Forget the food; give me the toy." However, when I opened the box, I discovered that the novelty item had to be assembled. (I should have known I was in trouble when the lady in the next booth leaned over and said, "Good luck!") It looked simple enough. Besides, no plastic toy is going to get the best of me! Five minutes must have passed with an anxious three-year-old looking on. But something seemed wrong about my finished product. All the moving parts moved—but in the wrong direction. At that point I thought it might be a good idea to read the directions

for assembly. Soon the toy was in good shape; and
again I realized the truth of that wise saying, "When all
else fails, read the instructions!"

I suppose that we all have experienced the horror of
extra parts, broken parts, and useless parts because we
failed to follow directions. Even David encountered
probems because he did not "read the instructions." He
was robbed of his joy; he lost a good man; and he was
forced to set aside his personal plans for three months.
Yet the problems he faced made him examine the
"instructions" very carefully.

The Journeys of the Ark (6:1-5)

From the parallel account of this incident in the
Chronicles, we learn that David held a council with the
captains and leaders of Israel (I Chronicles 13:1-4).
David assembled all of the Israelites for the purpose of
bringing the ark of God to Jerusalem. During Saul's
reign, the ark had not been revered as a symbol of
God's presence. The new king wanted a return of the
presence of God and a seeking of God's wisdom. This
suggestion pleased the elders; and a company of thirty
thousand religious leaders, musicians, officials, and
mighty men came to Baale (or Kirjath-jearim) to
accompany the ark to its new home (II Samuel 6:1-2).

For approximately seventy years the ark had been
kept in the home of Abinadab. It had arrived there in a
roundabout way. The Israelites had removed the ark
from Shiloh and attempted to make it a "good-luck
charm" against the Philistines (I Samuel 4:3). This
attitude displeased the Lord, who allowed the Israelites
to suffer defeat and the ark to be captured (I Samuel
4:10-11). The Philistines set the ark in their pagan
temple at Ashdod (I Samuel 5:1). However, when God

began to afflict the people with bubonic plague, they sent the ark to various Philistine cities. After seven months of disease, these coastal people had had enough (I Samuel 6:1). As quickly as possible they built a cart to which they yoked two cows. The ark was placed upon the cart, and the cows brought the precious cargo to Beth-shemesh (I Samuel 6:12). However, the men of this town looked into the ark, and many were killed because of their irreverence (I Samuel 6:19).

Therefore, the ark was sent to Kirjath-jearim, where Levites maintained it (I Samuel 7:1). Now David wanted the ark moved to Jerusalem, the new capital. This would make the city the religious center as well as the political center of the nation.

Similar to the Philistines' actions, a new cart was built for transporting the ark (II Samuel 6:3). Two sons of Abinadab, Uzzah and Ahio, were chosen to oversee the cart. The context appears to imply that Ahio led the cart while Uzzah followed it (6:4). As the journey began, the atmosphere was charged with excitement. David and the musicians praised God in song upon the instruments (6:5).

The Judgment Against Uzzah (6:6-11)

Ascending the hills to Jerusalem, one can encounter a rocky road. As the cart passed Nachon's threshingfloor, the oxen stumbled and shook the ark (6:6; cf. I Chronicles 13:9). The Hebrew word for *"shook"* means "to let loose or let drop." The ark was in danger of dropping to the ground and being damaged. In an expected reaction, Uzzah reached out to stabilize the ark (6:6). When he did so, God's *"anger . . . was kindled."* That phrase is one of intensive anger. God's holiness had been violated, and judgment was swift. Uzzah was

struck dead *"for his error"* (6:7). The word *"error"* occurs
only here in the entire Old Testament. It probably
means "for his hastiness." In his hastiness Uzzah had
forgotten to reverence God. How easy it is to allow
circumstances to dictate our action and in our hastiness
forget to honor our Lord!

When David realized what had happened, he also was
angered (KJV, *"displeased"*—6:8). His anger was not
against the Lord but against himself for obviously
displeasing the Lord. But an important lesson was
learned. *"And David was afraid of the Lord that day"* (6:9).
David caught a fresh vision of the holiness of God, and
that provoked him to ask, *"How shall the ark of the Lord come
to me?"* (6:9). In other words, he was asking, "If God
won't meet with me on my terms, then how can I
experience His presence?" Three months would pass
before David could answer that question (6:11). That is
how long the ark was left in the house of Obed-edom
(6:10-11). During that brief interlude, Obed-edom and
his family were blessed by the presence of the ark of
God.

To find out what David did during those three
months, we must examine the insights of the aged
chronicler. A building project was continuing in
Jerusalem. Houses were being constructed; but more
importantly, a place for the ark of God was being
prepared (I Chronicles 15:1). Along with this physical
preparation came a spiritual preparation on the part of
the king. This is implied by the public statement of the
king, *"None ought to carry the ark of God but the Levites: for them
hath the Lord chosen to carry the ark of God, and to minister unto
him for ever"* (I Chronicles 15:2). How did he find that out?
The king must have been reading the Law of Moses
(Numbers 4:15). Four hundred years earlier God had
delivered a divine "job description" for Israel's king.

Contained in it was the command to write and read the law so that the king might obey the law of God (Deuteronomy 17:18-20). When all else fails, read the instructions! David did so and discovered three pre-requisites for blessing—prepared hearts (I Chronicles 15:1-2), proper methods (I Chronicles 15:13), and pure lives (I Chronicles 15:12, 14).

The Jubilation of David (6:12-19)

With renewed hope David returned to the house of Obed-edom, surrounded by thousands of expectant Israelites. A new joy was evidenced (6:13)—a joy which came through obedience. The Levites took up the ark on their shoulders and marched six steps (6:13). At that point they stopped and offered sacrifices to God for His help and blessing (cf. I Chronicles 15:26).

The praise continued as David danced (literally, "whirled") in jubilation, and the Levites glorified God in song. Shouting and music were to be heard as well. Finally, the procession arrived in Jerusalem, and the ark was placed in the tabernacle (6:17). After more burnt offerings had been presented, a psalm of thanksgiving was chanted (I Chronicles 16:7-36). Gifts of food were given to the people, and all went to their homes to rejoice (6:19).

The Jeering of Michal (6:16, 20-23)

When David came home, however, there was no rejoicing. Have you ever been really excited about something, only to come home and have cold water dumped on your enthusiasm? Michal had been observing from the window as David danced through the streets of Jerusalem (6:16), *"and she despised him in her*

heart." The word *"despise"* means "to hold in contempt or
to accord little worth to something." Michal saw little
value in praising God and, therefore, little value in
David or his actions. As soon as the king walked in the
door, he was met with ridicule. With tongue in cheek,
Michal proclaimed, *"How glorious was the king of Israel today"*
(6:20). Then she revealed her own problem. "You acted
like a fool. You should not have done such humiliating
things." There it is. Michal was so filled with pride that
she did not recognize the importance of humility.

David's response is beautiful. Allow me to paraphrase his words. "I wasn't doing it for you; I was doing
it for God" (6:21). David was saying, "Let me enjoy my
relationship with my Lord." Then he reaffirmed that he
would continue to humble (KJV, *"be base"*) himself and
even *"be more vile."* This last phrase signifies a lowering
of one's social status. David was not an image builder.
He wanted to be identified with the common slaves
(6:22). That is true greatness!

Because of her proud heart and rebellious self-will,
Michal was made childless for the rest of her life (6:23).
To be barren *("fruitless")* was a reproach among the
Eastern peoples. Michal's failure to enter into her
husband's joy cost her a special relationship with the
king and any children they might have had.

Let's summarize what we have learned in several
practical principles. First, you can do the right thing in
the wrong way and miss all the benefits. That's what
David did on his first attempt to move the ark. Second,
if we are to enjoy God's presence and power, we must
meet with God on His terms, not ours. Third, our personal relationship with God and expression of praise
must be pleasing to God, not men. And fourth—don't
forget—when all else fails, read the instructions!

TIMELESS TRUTHS FOR TODAY

1. You can do the right thing in the wrong way and miss all the benefits.

2. If we are to enjoy God's presence and power, we must meet with God on His terms, not ours.

3. Our personal relationship with God and our expression of praise must be pleasing to God, not men.

4. When all else fails, read the instructions!

Chapter 8

When God Says "No"
II Samuel 7:1-29

Scene one: A young girl sits in a lonely room, thinking of the circumstances that have recently come to pass. Plans had been in the works for months for a wedding with the boy of her dreams; but seemingly out of nowhere, conflicts arose and there will be no wedding.

Scene two: For years a man has worked hard and performed his job well. Climbing the ladder of success has not been easy. Finally, the opportunity comes for which he has been waiting. The position he has always wanted becomes available. Although he is in line for the promotion, a kid right out of college nudges him aside and shatters his dreams.

Scene three: The waiting room outside the doctor's office has been filled with tension, fears, and questions. The name is called and a young couple nervously walk through the door to hear the results of the tests. At the marriage altar they expected a full, rich, happy life to be theirs. Then a lump appeared. Sitting down, the doctor confirms their worst fears. Within six months these two would say "good-bye."

Literally thousands of similar scenes could be played before our eyes. One common thread weaves its way through the fabric of these stories. God has said "no" to their plans and dreams. David, too, had big dreams. His dreams revolved around doing something great for the God who had been so good to him. He even got tentative approval from God's spokesman, but his hopes were soon dashed against the breakers of God's will. David's submission to the ways of God exhibits for us the attitude we must have when God says "no."

The Proposal of David (7:1-3)

The kingdom had been united. Jerusalem had been taken. The Philistines had been defeated. David sat in a beautiful new palace that was built especially for him by Hiram, King of Tyre (7:2). He considered the goodness of God in giving him rest from fighting his enemies (7:1). He recalled the joy he and his kingdom had just experienced as the ark was brought to its new home in Jerusalem. Then the thought struck him, "Here I sit in a luxurious home while the ark reposes in that drab tent. God deserves better." The plan began to formulate.

For the first time we are introduced to the prophet Nathan. This man will later record many of the events surrounding David's life (I Chronicles 29:29). Since Nathan was God's spokesman for the kingdom, David decided to bounce a new idea off him. "Nathan, I'm troubled that I have a nicer house than the ark does" (7:2). Implied in the statement was that a new, majestic home should be provided for God's presence.

You must remember that Nathan was human—like the rest of us. The proposal sounded great to him. He would have a new "church" in which to preach. Quickly, he responded, *"Go, do all that is in thine heart; for the Lord is with thee" (7:3)*. How did Nathan know? He had not even talked to God about it. Maybe he reasoned as many of us do, "If it's in the name of God, it must be okay."

The Promise of God (7:4-17)

Have you ever stuck your foot in your mouth? Leaves a bad taste, doesn't it? Ask Nathan. That night as Nathan lay down to sleep, God spoke to him (7:4). He realized that he had spoken too soon. Now he would have to face David and admit he had been wrong.

Although God said "no" to David's desire, He never once condemned it. In fact, David was commended (II Chronicles 6:8). Nor was Nathan rebuked for his hasty approval. God understands our motives and teaches us gently.

What follows is one of the most important sections in all of God's Word. We call it the Davidic Covenant. (See the chart on Covenants on page 67.) Rather than David building a house for God, God promised to build a house for David. God's refusal to let David build a house for the ark was based upon four reasons. First, no precedent had been established (7:6). God had never dwelt in a "permanent" building, only a tent. Second, no request had been made by God for such a house (7:7). These plans were David's initiative, not God's. Third, no man of war could build this house (I Chronicles 22:8; 28:3). This was to be a house of peace. Fourth, no safety for the ark could yet be assured since Jerusalem was not fully fortified against her enemies (I Kings

5:3-4). All of that makes sense, unless it is your idea that has just been shot down. David could have felt empty. God knew that, and so He decided to give the king a reminder from the past and a glimpse of the future.

In essence God said, "Don't be disappointed. Look how far you've come—from a shepherd to a sovereign; from leading a flock of sheep to leading God's people (7:8). And haven't you enjoyed My presence with you over the years as we've walked through the valleys and up to the mountaintop (7:9a)? What about the enemies you have had to face? Didn't I help you conquer them all (7:9b)? Now you sit as undisputed king in Jerusalem. Your name has become great. Are you still disappointed?"

God did not stop there. The curtain of time was folded back, and the prospects were awesome. Five promises were made to David and Israel.

1. A Promise of Residency. *"Moreover I will appoint a place for my people Israel, and will plant them, that they may dwell in a place of their own, and move no more" (7:10a).*

2. A Promise of Security. *"Neither shall the children of wickedness afflict them any more, as beforetime" (7:10b).*

3. A Promise of Posterity. *"The Lord telleth thee that he will make thee an house" (7:11). "I will set up thy seed after thee" (7:12).*

4. A Promise of Authority. *"I will establish the throne of his kingdom for ever" (7:13).*

5. A Promise of Perpetuity. *"Thy kingdom shall be established for ever before thee" (7:16).*

Ultimately these promises are fulfilled in Jesus Christ. Christ is of the house of David (Matthew 1:1; Luke

3:31) and will subdue all enemies (I Corinthians 15:25), sitting upon the throne of David (Acts 2:29-30) and ruling a literal, earthly kingdom (Revelation 20:4-6; 21:1-8).

But what about a house for the ark? God did not forget. To David He said, *"And when thy days be fulfilled, and thou shalt sleep with thy fathers, I will set up thy seed after thee, which shall proceed out of thy bowels, and I will establish his kingdom. He shall build an house for my name" (7:12-13).* There it is. Solomon would build the temple.

The Prayer and Praise of David (7:18-29)

David was left speechless. Quickly he entered the tent of meeting to commune with God. The Scripture states simply that he *"sat before the Lord" (7:18).* The word *"sat"* also means "to tarry, to linger." David was not in a hurry. He searched for appropriate words. The promises had not bloated him; they had humbled him. Look at his expressions. *"Who am I?" (7:18). "What is my house?" (7:18). "What can David say more unto thee?" (7:20).* That's the way we should always approach God. Then David thanked the Lord for revealing these promises to him and praised Him for His greatness (7:21-24). This ends the first part of David's prayer.

Part two of the prayer is an earnest plea for God to fulfill what He had said (7:25-29). David found it hard to believe that he could be the subject of such abounding grace. David was very great, but he was also very human.

What simple truths can we glean from this deeply theological chapter? Three principles are especially applicable for us today. The first is: No matter how great our desires are to glorify God, they are always eclipsed by God's desires to glorify us. David wanted to do a great work for God, but God wanted to do a greater work in David. The second principle is this: The blessings of God should never cause us to be arrogant but appreciative. Because God had been so good to him, David said, *"Therefore hath thy servant found in his heart to pray this prayer unto thee"* (7:27). Last, but certainly not least: When God says "No," He always gives us something better. David dreamed big, but reality was bigger. Has God recently said "no" to you? Be alert! God's greatest blessings may be just around the corner.

TIMELESS TRUTHS FOR TODAY

1. No matter how great our dreams are to glorify God, they are always eclipsed by God's desires to glorify us.

2. The blessings of God should never cause us to be arrogant but appreciative.

3. When God says "No," He always gives us something better.

MAJOR COVENANTS OF SCRIPTURE
(A brief survey of the major covenants—their provisions and implications)

Covenant Title	Statement of the Covenant	Provisions of the Covenant	Fulfillment in Christ
Edenic	Genesis 1:28-30 2:16-17	Population of the Earth Domination of God's Creation Separation from the Tree of Knowledge of Good and Evil	Christ as the Second Adam I Corinthians 15:45-49 Romans 5:15-21
Adamic	Genesis 3:14-19	Destruction of Satan Salvation Through the Woman's Seed Affliction Through Childbirth	Christ as the Seed of the Woman Galatians 4:4
Noahic	Genesis 8:20—9:27	Government Established Judgment by Flood Ended	Christ as the Saviour from Destruction II Peter 3:3-9
Abrahamic	Genesis 12:1-3 13:14-17 15:1-18	A Nation Constituted Blessings Communicated Oppressors Cursed A Redeemer Confirmed	Christ as the Seed of Abraham Galatians 3:16
Mosaic	Exodus 19:5 20:1—31:18	Commandments to Obey Judgments on Those Who Disobey	Christ as the Satisfaction of the Requirements of the Law Matthew 3:15; 5:17 I John 2:2
Palestinian	Deuteronomy 30:1-10	Dispersion Among the Nations Conversion of the People Restoration to the Land Expansion of the Blessings	Christ as the Surety of the Inheritance Colossians 1:12-14
Davidic	II Samuel 7:5-19	Family Posterity (a house) Royal Authority (a throne) National Perpetuity (a kingdom)	Christ as the Sovereign Who Will Reign (The Seed of David) Luke 1:31-33
New	Hebrews 8:7-12	Revelation of the Law Relationship with God Redemption from Sin	Christ as the Sacrifice Who Establishes the New Covenant Jeremiah 31:31-34 Matthew 26:26-29

Chapter 9

Conquering New Frontiers
II Samuel 8:1-18

"Hard times." I suppose everyone has his own definition of that phrase with a full complement of illustrations to prove his point. David had gone through some "hard times," and you would think that the worst would now be over. God had just promised him a great and everlasting kingdom (II Samuel 7). Chapter eight unfolds for us the expanding of David's empire through devastating victories over his border enemies. All of it sounds so easy as we read through the narrative, but war is never easy. Overcoming the enemy is not a simple task. The path of victory is haunted by the grotesque demons of doubt, distress, and despair. A psalm from the pen of David reveals some of the inward struggles with skepticism that he faced during the battles in this period of his life. Listen to these words: *"O God, thou hast cast us off, thou hast scattered us . . . Thou hast shewed thy people hard things"* (Psalm 60:1, 3). Hard things . . . hard times . . . they're both hard to handle. But long ago David had come to grips with the truth that *"the battle is the Lord's"* (I Samuel 17:47). In his hour of conflict he returned to that truth: *"Through God we shall do valiantly: for he it is that shall tread down our enemies"* (Psalm 60:12). David could have thrown up his hands in hopelessness and said, "What's the use?" That's what most of us do. Instead of expanding our frontiers of influence, we are satisfied with a powerless, two-by-four kingdom. David knew that either he would conquer his enemies or they would conquer him. He chose the former, and God blessed him for it.

The Assault on David's Enemies (8:1-14)

"And after this . . . David smote . . . and subdued them" (8:1). This historian of II Samuel puts the eighth chapter in perspective with the phrase, *"And after this."* After what? After God's promise to build a kingdom for David and after David's communion with God for a long period, the king went forth to defeat his enemies. He was virtually surrounded by nations who had plagued Israel. To the west was Philistia. To the east was Moab. To the north were the men of Zobah and the Aramaeans. To the south were the Edomites. Systematically, David attacked every potential threat in order to insure peace and prosperity for his own people. Bear in mind that chapter eight takes place over a period of time. Perhaps the events of II Samuel 10 are an enlargement of one of these conflicts. In David's victories we find the importance of confronting and conquering our enemies in our spiritual warfare.

David first turned eastward to the age-old nemesis, Philistia. The Philistines were not completely annihilated, but they were subdued. The Arabic cognate for this word means "to fold" in one's hand as folding the wings of a bird. The implication is that the Philistines would no longer be free to assail their foe. In the conflict with this western kingdom, David took Methegammah, which was another name for Gath (I Chronicles 18:1). *"Metheg-ammah"* means "bridle of the mother." Gath had become the preeminent city of Philistia and controlled the area as a bridle controls a horse. However, David took the reins and brought Philistia under his control.

Next, the Israelite monarch turned to the east against Moab (8:2). At one time David had been on good terms with Moab. His great-grandmother, Ruth, was a Moabitess. Also, he had even left his parents there when fleeing from Saul (I Samuel 22:3-4). But more than fifteen years had passed, and animosity had developed. Some Jewish writers believe that David's parents had been slain in Moab. If this were true, it might explain the brutality of David's men. The soldiers of Moab were forced to lie on the ground. Then in a mass execution, two thirds of the army were put to death. The remaining third became David's servants and paid tribute regularly.

Turning his attention northward, David marched his troops against the kingdom of Zobah and its allies (8:3). Saul had also encountered these forces during his reign (I Samuel 14:47). This kingdom was located north of Damascus in an area that we know as Syria. These hostilities may have grown out of the war with Ammon (II Samuel 10:6). The passage implies that Hadadezer, the king of Zobah, had suffered a serious setback because he attempted *"to recover his border at the river Euphrates" (8:3)*. In the second battle Israel took one thousand chariots, seven thousand horsemen, and twenty thousand infantry as captives (I Chronicles

18:4). It is amazing that the Israelites could defeat their enemies in such a resounding way since they did not rely on chariots and horses. God had warned them not to trust in horses but in the Lord (Deuteronomy 17:16). The temptation to retain the war horses must have been great, but David had all except one hundred hamstrung (KJV, *"houghed"*). Later David would write, *"Some trust in chariots, and some in horses: but we will remember the name of the Lord our God" (Psalm 20:7).*

When the Aramaeans (KJV, *"Syrians"*) of Damascus heard the news, they came *"to succour Hadadezer" (8:5).* The Hebrew uses a play on words. *"To succour"*—meaning "to help"—comes from the Hebrew word *'ezer* (a word which is also contained in this king's name). *"Hadadezer"* means "whose help is Hadad." Hadad was the sun-god worshiped by the people of Zobah. But his sun-god was powerless against God Almighty. Therefore, the Aramaeans had "to help him whose help is Hadad." A lot of help they were! Twenty-two thousand of their army were killed. Fortifying his frontiers, David stationed garrisons of soldiers among the Aramaeans.

At this point the writer tells us what we have so far assumed: *"And the Lord preserved David whithersoever he went" (8:6; see also 8:14).* The word *"preserve"* also means "to save, deliver, help." (Contrast Hadad's help with the Lord's.) The Arabic root for this word means "to make wide." By overcoming his enemies, David was able to experience a new freedom. His foes had restricted him, but his faith and fighting opened up new frontiers. Spiritual enemies bind our influences, too. Yet when we fight the good fight of faith, God will be our help to defeat our enemies and give us a new freedom to serve Him (Romans 6:11-14, 17-22).

The kingdom of Zobah had enjoyed great prosperity. Its soldiers bore shields of gold (8:7). These David saved and brought to Jerusalem and dedicated them to God. From other cities David seized large amounts of bronze (8:8). Why did David save these treasures? Was he selfishly hoarding such wealth in disobedience to God (Deuteronomy 17:17)? The answer is found in two verses. I Kings 7:51 reveals that the gold and silver were placed as the Lord's treasure in Solomon's temple. I Chronicles 18:8 says that the bronze was used for *"the brasen sea, and the pillars, and the vessels of brass"* in Solomon's temple. God had said "no" to David concerning the construction of a temple, but this man had not lost his vision or love for God. David actually played an important part in the building of the temple. He prepared the way (I Chronicles 22).

Approximately one hundred miles north of Damascus in the town of Hamath lived another king named Toi (8:9). He had been at odds with Hadadezer for some time. News of David's victory pleased him; so he sent his son Joram (or Hadoram) to bless him and give him gifts (8:10). These gifts were dedicated to the Lord along with the other spoil (8:11). This reminds us how pleased God is when we defeat our enemies; and His Son, the Exalted One (Joram means "exalted"), gives us greater gifts to use for His glory.

However, the fighting was not over. The title and first five verses of Psalm 60 seem to indicate that Edom attacked Israel's southern borders while David's men engaged their enemies to the north. As quickly as they could, Israel assembled in the Valley of Salt just south of the Dead Sea (8:13). The Edomites lost eighteen thousand men in the battle. Joab, David's captain, remained in the land of Edom, killing every male (I Kings 11:15-17). One royal male, the child Hadad, escaped to Egypt. Later, he would return to be a thorn in Solomon's side. The conquest of Edom was important because it gave Israel the control over southern trade routes, provided them with copper mines, and established an access to the Gulf of Aqaba, where the port city of Ezion-geber would be built.

The Administration of David's Empire (8:15-18)

With the borders expanded and secured in all directions, David ruled safely over all Israel. His reign was characterized by the execution of *"judgment and justice" (8:15)*. *"Judgment"* is primarily a secular, political word and speaks of the entire process of government— legislative, executive, and judicial. In dealing with the people, David established just laws, executed proper procedures, and enforced what was right. *"Justice"* would be better translated as "righteousness." This is a religious word and speaks of a conformity to an ethical, moral standard. (See the usage of this word in Leviticus 19:15 and Proverbs 14:34.) Justice ("righteousness") was the basis for good judgment ("government"). Because there were moral, godly standards, the kingdom became strong.

Of course, a nation like Israel also needed good organization and competent leaders. David had carefully selected his men. Joab was captain over the armies (8:16). He had earned this position by taking Jerusalem. Jehoshaphat was the recorder (8:16). He kept the written records of the king and kingdom. This would include setting appointments and organizing the staff. Zadok and Ahimelech were the priests ministering before the ark (8:17). Seraiah was the scribe (8:17). Seraiah's duties may have included diplomatic functions (cf. Isaiah 36:3) and conscriptions for the military (cf. II Kings 25:19). He was possibly similar to our Secretary of State. Benaiah was over the Cherethites and the Pelethites. These two groups served as the king's bodyguards. The Cherethites may have been executioners, while the Pelethites were runners or couriers. Then came David's sons. They were chief advisors to the king (I Chronicles 18:17). Other of his administration will be introduced in succeeding chapters.

Several applications can be drawn from the chapter. First, true freedom comes not from doing what you want but from doing as you should. David was undoubtedly tired of fighting, but without conflict there is no crown. The second truth is that we must "put to death" everything that could lead us to misplaced confidence. David hamstrung the horses so that he would not be tempted to trust in them rather than God. Third, we must recognize that God will always bring to pass the promises of His Word. The destruction of Moab was a fulfillment of Numbers 24:17. The subduing of Edom was a fulfillment of Genesis 25:22-23. The conquest to the Euphrates was a partial fulfillment of the Abrahamic Covenant (Genesis 15:18). As David saw God's promises fulfilled before his eyes, do you suppose he thought about God's promise to him in chapter seven? And fourth, our spiritual impact on future generations is determined by our spiritual triumphs under the present circumstances. Because David conquered his enemies and stored up treasures for God's glory, he had a dynamic influence upon his son, upon Solomon's kingdom, and upon the temple which Solomon built. What will be your impact on the next generation?

TIMELESS TRUTHS FOR TODAY

1. True freedom does not come from doing what you want but from doing as you should.

2. "Put to death" everything that will cause misplaced confidence.

3. God will always fulfill His promises.

4. Your spiritual impact on future generations is determined by your spiritual triumphs under present circumstances.

10

Amazing Grace!

II Samuel 9:1-13

The year was 1725 when a godly mother gave birth to her only child, a boy. Like Hannah in the Old Testament, she dedicated this child to the Lord, praying that he would one day occupy a pulpit in their native land of England. As the boy grew, this faithful mother instructed him in the Bible, the Westminster Catechism, and the children's hymns of Isaac Watts. But tragically, the mother died when the lad was six years old. Soon the father, who lacked any spiritual zeal, married a woman who had no spiritual concerns either. The life of the child was all downhill. He was sent away to boarding school but dropped out to become a sailor like his father. Turning from God, he embraced libertine philosophies that wrecked his life. Drinking, profanity, rebellion, and sensuality gripped him, choking out all desire to serve God. He even repudiated the God of his mother. He ran from responsibility, deserted the Royal Navy, and ultimately found himself a servant of slaves on the west coast of Africa. His body became racked with pain and illness. Life did not seem worth living.

Somehow he managed to contact his father and informed him of his desire to come home. One of the father's friends was about to set sail for Africa on the ship, *Greyhound.* When the young man arrived at Sierra Leone, the captain arranged to bring him home. While returning, a fierce storm arose. So violent was the tempest that the crew was certain the ship would sink. In that hour of desperation the wayward man cried out for mercy, but then in despair he rationalized that there could be no mercy for such a wretch as he. He began to read the Bible and found that there was hope for the worst of sinners. By faith he came to trust Christ and became a new creature. Nearly sixteen years later he was ordained as a minister of the Gospel and faithfully proclaimed God's Word in several pulpits. In later years he reflected on his misery in sin and the greatness of God's love in saving him. The man's name was John Newton. His reflections are recorded in one of our beloved hymns.

> Amazing grace! how sweet the sound,
> That saved a wretch like me!
> I once was lost, but now am found,
> Was blind, but now I see.
>
> Through many dangers, toils, and snares,
> I have already come;
> 'Tis grace hath brought me safe thus far,
> And grace will lead me home.

What can take a wretched infidel like John Newton and transform him into an influential servant of God? Only God's amazing grace! II Samuel 9 contains a story of just such amazing grace, and it pictures for us a God of mercy reaching down and touching the lives of wretches like you and me.

A Promise Remembered (9:1-4)

Similar to the beginning of Chapter 7, David was again home from fighting. In the first instance (II Samuel 7) he thought of the Lord; this time he thought of others. His mind resurrected the memory of a dear friend—Jonathan (9:1). Years before, David had made a covenant that he would show kindness to Jonathan's children (I Samuel 20:14-15). (A comparable promise was made to Saul. See I Samuel 24:20-22.) The king began to inquire if any descendant of Saul and Jonathan had survived the Philistine wars and their aftermath. Since none of David's court officials knew for sure, they called Ziba, a former servant of Saul (9:2). He informed the king of at least one remaining son of Jonathan's, but he was lame (9:3)—not the kind of fellow desired around a palace. He had suffered from a fall and was a cripple (II Samuel 4:4). Perhaps to everyone's surprise, David asked of his whereabouts (9:4). Ziba knew where he was, which causes us to question why this servant of Saul was not performing his responsibility to Saul's house. He might have despised this cripple (cf. 9:3) and have seen no opportunity for rewards in serving him. Nevertheless, the king was told, *"He is in the house of Machir, the son of Ammiel, in Lo-debar" (9:4)*. Machir must have been a wealthy man. II Samuel 17:27-29 reveals that Machir was one of the men who provided David and his men food and supplies when he fled from Absalom. (This act of kindness might have been prompted by David's kindness to Jonathan's son.) Machir lived in Lo-debar, a city of Gilead believed to have been located ten miles south of the Sea of Galilee in the Transjordan area.

Several spiritual parallels are evident thus far. The king wanted to demonstrate kindness to someone on the merits of another. When the object of that kindness was discovered, he was in a far-off place. Although Machir's house was filled with pleasures, it also symbolized bondage. "*Machir*" means "sold." In the New Testament Paul reminds us that the sinner is in bondage, *"sold under sin"* *(Romans 7:14)*. The city of residence was called *"Lo-debar,"* meaning "no pasture." It was a place of little substance and little growth. Barrenness typified the area. Worst of all, Jonathan's son had been crippled by a fall. This made him incapable of doing many things for himself. He had been marred for life.

A Privilege Received (9:5-6, 8)

Immediately David sent to Lo-debar for this lame man (9:5). His name was Mephibosheth ("he who spreads shame"). The custom in the Eastern cultures was that the king of any new dynasty would destroy all relatives from the previous ruling family. This would tend to stabilize the new monarch by eliminating potential opposition. For years Mephibosheth had lived in relative obscurity. He had been brought to the Transjordan area by his nurse when he was five. Now he was old enough to have a son of his own (cf. 9:12). Mephibosheth might have lived all those years in fear of what David might do to him. When the delegation from David came to Machir's house, Mephibosheth wrestled with anxiety and panic. What would happen in Jerusalem?

Upon arriving at Jerusalem, the former prince was granted the privilege of standing before the king. In David's presence he humbly prostrated himself and honored the one who controlled his fate. He even labeled himself as David's servant (9:6). Then David revealed his gracious plans to Mephibosheth. This crippled man could hardly believe his ears. Again he bowed himself but was unable to comprehend such grace. *"What is thy servant, that thou shouldest look upon such a dead dog as I am?" (9:8)*. The allusion to a *"dead dog"* was to an animal of contempt in that society (cf. I Samuel 17:43; Matthew 7:6). Mephibosheth's statement may have reminded David of a similar statement that he had made to Saul (I Samuel 24:14). Mephibosheth realized that he did not deserve such mercies and privileges.

A Position Restored (9:7, 9-13)

David said, *"I will surely shew thee kindness for Jonathan thy father's sake" (9:7)*. The word *"kindness"* occurs three times in this chapter (9:1, 3, 7). In the second instance it is defined as *"the kindness of God" (9:3)*. The Greek version almost always translated this word "mercy." The Hebrew word contains the ideas of love, goodness, loyalty, and faithfulness and identifies one of God's basic attributes (Exodus 20:6). Also included in the word is the concept of forgiveness (Exodus 34:6-7). David's action would be one of mercy to the undeserving, an act of forgiveness to the ruthless Saul, and an act of love to a departed friend. Such kindness could only be demonstrated by a man after God's own heart.

The kindness of the king resulted in several benefits. First, all of the lands owned by Saul would be returned to Mephibosheth (9:7). In his fall and while fleeing, he had lost the rights of his inheritance. The enemy had taken control of the territory. But David had paid the price to win back those lands, and he now presented them as a gift of grace. The second benefit was that Mephibosheth would eat bread at the king's table continually (9:7, 10, 11, 13). The use of the word *"continually"* indicates the permanency of the relationship. The quality of the relationship is manifested in a third benefit: Mephibosheth was to be *"as one of the king's sons" (9:11)*.

This lame young man had lost his position as a prince.
David restored that place of honor. Fourth, the king
ordered Ziba, his sons, and his servants to serve Mephibosheth (9:9-10) since Mephibosheth did not have power
in himself to work the land and produce fruit. But with
Ziba's fifteen sons and twenty servants as helpers, he
would be able to enjoy a prosperous, fruitful life. Fifth,
Mephibosheth would take his residency with the king in
the palace at Jerusalem (9:13).

Imagine how Mephibosheth must have welled up
with joy when he heard these things! Although no
words of thanks are recorded, you can be sure that he
had a grateful heart. Maybe the meaning of his son's
name, Micha, expressed his sincere appreciation best:
"Who is like Jehovah?" Only God in His grace can reach
out and reverse circumstances like Mephibosheth's.

The story can be summed up simply. David looked for
anybody, found a *nobody*, and made him a *somebody*. And
that's what God can do for the sinner. We were all
destroyed by "the fall" and became outcasts from the
kingdom (Romans 3:23). But as David sought for
Mephibosheth, so Jesus Christ came to seek and to save
that which was lost (Luke 19:10). When we fall down
before the King of kings and trust Him, we receive a new
life. Old things are passed away; all things become new.
In Mephibosheth's case one thing did not change. He
was always lame; this condition served as a constant
reminder of his former state and God's amazing grace.
Do you feel like a nobody? God can make you a somebody if you humbly bow before the King of kings. We
have all been crippled by sin, but those who trust Christ
are privileged to be called sons.

TIMELESS TRUTHS FOR TODAY

1. God's grace is available to everyone.

2. God's grace can change anyone.

3. God's grace can make you a someone.

84

PARALLELS BETWEEN MEPHIBOSHETH AND
THE SINNER SAVED BY GRACE

MEPHIBOSHETH	THE SINNER
Mephibosheth was crippled by the fall. II Samuel 4:4	The sinner "fell" in Adam. Genesis 3:1-7; Romans 5:12
Mephibosheth lived in the house of Machir ("sold"). II Samuel 9:4	The sinner is *"sold under sin."* Romans 7:14
Mephibosheth lived in Lo-debar ("no pasture"). II Samuel 9:4	The sinner's life is barren.
Mephibosheth was shown kindness for Jonathan's sake. II Samuel 9:1	The sinner has grace demonstrated for Jesus' sake. Ephesians 2:4,5,8; Titus 3:4-5
Mephibosheth was sought by the king. II Samuel 9:5	The sinner is sought by the King of kings. Luke 19:10
Mephibosheth humbled himself before the king. II Samuel 9:6	The sinner must humble himself before God. Matthew 18:3-4; Philippians 2:9-11
Mephibosheth saw himself as undeserving (*"a dead dog"*). II Samuel 9:8	The sinner must recognize his sin. Romans 3:10; 3:23
Mephibosheth's land was restored. II Samuel 9:7	The saved sinner is given an inheritance. Colossians 1:12; 3:24
Mephibosheth sat at the king's table continually. II Samuel 9:7,10,11,13	The saved sinner sits in *"heavenly places."* Ephesians 1:3; 2:6
Mephibosheth was given servants to help. II Samuel 9:9-10	The saved sinner is given the Holy Spirit as the Helper. John 14:16
Mephibosheth was to see that fruit was produced. II Samuel 9:10	The saved sinner is to evidence the fruit of the Spirit. Galatians 5:22-23
Mephibosheth became as one of the king's sons (adoption). II Samuel 9:11	The saved sinner becomes a son of God (adoption). John 1:12; Romans 8:15
Mephibosheth lived in a prepared place in Jerusalem. II Samuel 9:13	The saved sinner has a prepared place in Heaven. John 14:2-3

11

Embarrassing Moments
II Samuel 10:1-19

The life and deeds of Plato have recently caught my interest. Not Plato, the philosopher, but Plato, the canine kleptomaniac. Estelle Mendelsohn tells the true story of the misadventures of her dalmatian in *Animals Can Be Almost Human.* It seems that Plato was totally unteachable in the useful art of serving his master. The one thing he could do was to fetch things. Regrettably, he only fetched things that did not belong to the Mendelsohn family. Often he would snatch stuffed animals from unguarded baby buggies. There was little reaction in the community until a desperate plea appeared in the classified section of the daily paper. Listen to Estelle relive the story.*

" 'Will the person who took white teddy bear from child's stroller please return it? Two-year-old owner is inconsolable.' The address given was some distance away. After a hurried family meeting, it was decided

that the head of the house should wait until dark and
then advance surreptitiously to the front door of the
place, deposit the teddy bear, and scram. After all, it
would be most embarrassing to have to admit that one
was the owner of a canine kleptomaniac.

This plan was carried out successfully, up to a point.
Unfortunately, the head of the house collided with a
wrought-iron chair. Whereupon a startled householder
switched on the porch lights and flung open the front
door. Plato's owner mumbled something about this
being the place, he thought, that had lost a teddy bear—
and fled down the walk. Not, however, before he heard a
voice, shrill with contempt, shouting, 'Boy! How low can
you sink—swiping babies' toys!' "

Embarrassing moments come in all shapes and sizes.
The incidents preserved for us in the tenth chapter of
II Samuel reveal how a good deed led to an embarrassing
moment which ultimately triggered a war between the
Ammonites and the men of Israel.

Reaction: Comforting Compassion (10:1-2)

The loss of a loved one can be a traumatic experience.
David had gone through that valley when he learned of
the death of his best friend, Jonathan. The valley grew
darker when his parents died. He knew the meaning of
suffering and loneliness. It is not surprising that when
he learned of the death of Nahash, King of Ammon, his
heart was touched and he was moved to action.

Nahash, who may be the same king mentioned in I
Samuel 11, had befriended David. Perhaps during
David's days as a fugitive, Nahash had assisted and
protected the young man. Such help would not be
unexpected if this were the Nahash who was Saul's
enemy. Many years had passed since the battle at

Jabesh-gilead, and the Ammonite king died at an old age (10:1).

In remembering the kindness of Nahash, David considered what he could do to comfort Nahash's son, Hanun (10:2). A group of Jewish officials was chosen to represent the king to Hanun. These officials would express their sorrow and grief to the bereaved prince on David's behalf.

Response: Cruel Contempt (10:3-5)

Suspicious of David's motives, some of Hanun's officers gathered to express their apprehensions. These leaders thought that Hanun was being duped into believing that David was truly honoring the deceased father by sending mourners (10:3). They convinced the king that David's envoy had other purposes—namely, *"to search the city"* (diligent probing to gather information), *"to spy it out"* (exploring the city on foot), *"and to overthrow it"* (conquering the city).

In response and retaliation to the suspected espionage, Hanun publicly humiliated David's ambassadors (10:4). First, he shaved off half of their beards (i.e., one side). James Freeman writes, "According to Oriental sentiment a greater indignity could not have been put upon them. The beard is considered a symbol of manhood, and, in some places, of freedom—slaves being compelled to shave their beards in token of servitude. By shaving half of their beards, Hanun not only treated David's ambassadors with contempt, but made them objects of ridicule . . . So disgraceful is it considered to have the beard cut off, that some of the Orientals would prefer death to such a punishment" (*Manners and Customs of the Bible*, pp.143-144). A second disgraceful act was committed against David's representatives when Hanun had their long robes cut off at the hip, literally exposing them to public shame.

David's men refused to return to Jerusalem in their condition. The account states that they were greatly ashamed (10:5). The word for *"ashamed"* means also "to reproach, hurt, or blush," conveying the idea of public humiliation. The Arabic cognate of this word speaks of a wounding of the spirit. Unable to stand the thought of facing anyone, the ambassadors fled to Jericho. While there, David encouraged the men and urged them to remain in the city of palms until their beards were grown.

Result: Catastrophic Conflict (10:6-19)

Soon it became evident that David would punish the Ammonites for their cruelty. The Ammonites realized *"that they stank before David" (10:6)*. The word *"stank"* is used figuratively of abhorrence, such as the reaction to the smell of something rotten. Being unable to field an army as strong as Israel's, the king of Ammon solicited help from his neighbors to the north. Twenty thousand Aramaeans (KJV, *"Syrians"*) from Beth-rehob and Zobah were enlisted along with a thousand soldiers from the king of Maacah and twelve thousand men from Tob. For their services they received one thousand talents of silver. Although the price of silver fluctuates, the enormous price paid for these mercenaries is apparent from the weight of the silver.

One talent equals approximately sixty-six thousand pounds or over one million ounces. That's a lot of pocket change! Looking at it from another perspective, one authority cites that a talent is equivalent to six thousand denarii. The payment would therefore be six million denarii. (In New Testament times a denarius was a day's wage.)

The northern forces pitched camp near Medeba (I Chronicles 19:7). Quickly David responded by sending Joab and his mighty men to confront the enemy (10:7). But Joab's armies were faced with having to battle on two fronts (10:8). Joab needed a successful strategy in order to defeat this confederation. Recognizing the relative weaknesses of the Ammonite troops, Joab chose his best men to initiate an offensive thrust against the Aramaeans (10:9). Abishai, Joab's brother, assumed command of the remaining Israelite forces, who would fight against the Ammonites (10:10). If the Aramaeans proved to be too strong for Joab, Abishai would lead a second wave of fresh soldiers to assist his brother. And if Abishai encountered unforeseen resistance, Joab would shore up the ranks with his men (10:11).

The hour of battle arrived, and Joab gathered his men for a final word (10:12). He asked them to be of good courage (prepare to fight for yourself) and to strengthen themselves, for the cities of their God (prepare to fight for your God). After this stirring challenge, he committed the conflict to the will of God—*"the Lord do that which seemeth him good"* (10:12).

From the very first engagement, the handwriting was on the wall. Joab completely dismantled the threat from the Aramaeans (10:13). When the Ammonites saw their allies suffering defeat, they retreated to their city (10:14). All that money was wasted! Victorious in this initial confrontation, Joab returned to Jerusalem to prepare and wait for a more suitable time of year for a siege. However, the Aramaeans were not about to give up. Under the leadership of Hadadezer (or Hadarezer), reinforcements from beyond the Euphrates were summoned (10:15-16; cf. 8:3-6)). This refurbished army gathered at Helam with Shobach serving as commander of the forces (10:16). The gravity of the situation is evident since David himself took command of this expedition, which included not only the mighty men but also all of the available fighting men (10:17). David prevailed and Shobach was killed in combat (10:18). The kings who had leagued themselves with Hadadezer hastily made peace with David, agreeing to serve him (10:19). The victory was important because it discouraged the Aramaeans from lending any more aid to the Ammonites.

Review: Closing Considerations

Three important truths stand out in this story. First, debts of kindness are to be repaid by acts of love. David was indebted to Nahash for his deeds of mercy in the time of need. When David was in a position to return this favor, he did so. Solomon must have learned this principle from his father, for he said, *"Withhold not good from them to whom it is due, when it is in the power of thine hand to do it" (Proverbs 3:27).* Second, acts of love may be misinterpreted and rejected by others. Hanun unwisely listened to his suspicious advisors, and it cost him dearly. Third, when rejection leads to conflict, do what you can to resolve the problem and leave the rest with God. Joab found himself in the middle of a huge "problem." He did not give up or give out. He formulated a plan of action (10:9-11), implemented it, and left the results in the hands of God.

Maybe your deeds of kindness have been rejected by others. Perhaps you are feeling the pressures of conflict. Take Joab's advice: "Be strong, encourage yourself to do what is right, and commit your ways unto the Lord." God will reward you with victory and peace.

TIMELESS TRUTHS FOR TODAY

1. Debts of kindness are to be repaid by acts of love.

2. Acts of love may be misinterpreted and rejected by others.

3. When rejection leads to conflict, do what you can to solve the problem and leave the rest with God.

Chapter 12

A Skeleton in the Closet
II Samuel 11:1-27

The human skeleton is a marvel of creation with its 206 distinct bones working in harmony to support the anatomy. A recent publication noted an interesting statistic that a well-preserved skeleton sold for $190 in 1976. Because of inflation, that rate rose to $475 in 1978. A year later a foot brought $26 while a skull with teeth intact could cost $140.

Skeletons can demand a high price. This is especially true of skeletons that are hidden in back closets. If we were honest, most of us would have to admit that we are harboring one or more skeletons from the past. Indeed, we would be willing to pay any amount to rid ourselves of these ghostly reminders. All too often, however, they haunt us throughout our lives. Our deepest prayer is that they might not be discovered by another.

Up to this period of his life, David had avoided any major mistakes. Certainly, he had had his problems, just as we all have; but his closets were relatively clean. Beginning with chapter eleven of II Samuel, however, things changed. An ugly blot stained the life of God's man. Unfortunately, David allowed himself the luxury of playing with fire and ended up with third-degree burns and scars that marred his image until his death.

Before we examine this lamentable experience in David's life, we must offer a word of caution. The temptation will arise to point an accusing finger at David or Bathsheba, to condemn and criticize. We might even pharisaically compare our sins to theirs and seek to justify ourselves or exalt our self-righteousness. Our purpose is to discover the reason for this sin, its descending road, and its tragic results in order that we might avoid the pitfalls of any sin. Paul offered some excellent advice when he wrote, *"Wherefore let him that thinketh he standeth take heed lest he fall"* (I Corinthians 10:12).

An Unguarded Moment (11:1-5)

The stage for David's sin is set for us in the tenth chapter. Hanun, King of the Ammonites, had humiliated a special envoy of mourners sent from David (10:4). The resulting tensions drew the two nations into war (10:6 ff). After the Aramaeans, allies of the Ammonites, had been defeated, the men of Ammon withdrew to safety within the walls of their city. The conflict might have taken place near the commencement of the rainy season, for Joab decided to return to Jerusalem to wait a more opportune time (10:14).

"And it came to pass, after the year was expired, at the time when kings go forth to battle" (11:1) establishes the time when Joab resumed his assault. The Hebrew literally says, "at the return of the year," which was in the springtime (the month of Nisan—March/April) when the latter rains

were ended. This was a suitable time for war since the weather would be less likely to interfere and provisions would be more abundant with the barley, wheat, and general harvests being made.

It was customary for kings to lead their men into battle during this period, as verse one implies. However, David resolved to stay in Jerusalem. Joab was sent to Ammon to settle the issue quickly. Although the walled city of Rabbah proved a difficult obstacle, Joab was able to demoralize the surrounding countryside in a series of raids (cf. I Chronicles 20:1). But Rabbah was ready for a lengthy siege. As someone has said, "While Joab laid siege against Rabbah, Satan laid siege against David."

Returning to Jerusalem, we view a dark episode in the life of David. This is the third time we have seen him alone in his capital. The first time (II Samuel 7), his thoughts turned to God. The second time (II Samuel 9), his thoughts turned to others. The third time (II Samuel 11), his thoughts turned to self. The sun was beginning to set on that cool, refreshing spring day. The fighting was far away. The only sounds in Jerusalem were the songs of birds and the laughter of children at play. The sweet fragrance of newly budding flowers filled the air as a relaxed king arose from his bed for a stroll upon the roof (11:2). With joy and perhaps a pinch of pride, he gazed over the growing city named after himself. However, as the darkness began to creep across the Judean hills, darkness began to creep across David's soul as he caught a glimpse of a young Jewish girl bathing in the evening.

Many commentators and preachers have condemned this girl for tempting the king. Although later Bathsheba might have been able to prevent what took place, it seems unjust to question this Jewess here. Without a doubt, she was washing herself in the courtyard of her home as was normal practice. She bathed herself at the usual time of day for such. One student of customs has observed that men who walked upon the rooftop in the evenings would purposefully look into the distance to avoid a temptation similar to that of David.

David probably was not looking for trouble. The accidental glance upon the woman was unavoidable. But David continued to stare. (The Hebrew word also means "to inspect.") Compounding the problem was the exceptional beauty of Bathsheba. The literal Hebrew says that she was "good of appearance, very." In our modern vernacular, she was a "looker." David's desires were aroused. Immediately he sent a servant to seek information about the woman (11:3). When the report came back that she was married to Uriah the Hittite, the matter should have ended there. God's law condemned coveting another man's wife (Exodus 20:17). Besides, Uriah was one of David's most loyal servants, being one of his *"mighty men" (II Samuel 23:39).*

What takes place next is a confirmation of the words of James: *"Every man is tempted, when he is drawn away of his own lust, and enticed. Then when lust hath conceived, it bringeth forth sin" (James 1:14-15).* David again sent his servants and invited Bathsheba to an audience with the king (11:4). David "saw"; he "inquired"; he "took." Those three steps are common to every sin. Before long the act had been committed, lives had been altered, and a skeleton was stuck in a closet. There is an irony in the story. In keeping with Mosaic Law, Bathsheba purified herself after the sexual relations and then returned home. It seems strange to disregard one command while obeying another; yet that is typical of Christians. Then within a few weeks Bathsheba sent word to David that must have shaken him. Bathsheba was bearing David's child (11:5).

What led to David's sin? No one ever accidentally
entertains thoughts and actions like these. Three
factors contributed to this downfall: incomplete obedience, inappropriate attitudes, and improper actions.
David had not obeyed God's law concerning multiplica-
tion of wives (Deuteronomy 17:17). He had also become embittered at Michal (II Samuel 6:20-23). Such
bitterness leads to sensuality (Hebrews 12:15-16). Finally, he allowed himself to be in a position of temptation by walking on the roof in the evening. The New
Testament warns, *"Make not provision for the flesh, to fulfil
the lusts thereof"* (Romans 13:14).

An Unsuccessful Maneuver (11:6-13)

Imagine the turmoil David must have been going
through in those moments. He had to make a choice.
Should he admit his failure or try to cover up? Being
afraid of confessing his guilt, he chose the latter.
Pretending to want a report of Joab's progress at
Rabbah, David sent for Uriah to give him a briefing
(11:6). Uncomfortably, the king sat with Uriah and
asked questions mechanically (11:7). After giving
answers that David never heard, Uriah was sent to his
house in the hope that he would have relations with his
wife and eliminate any suspicions about David (11:8).
The king also sent a feast of food to soothe further his
own conscience. But Uriah did something the king did
not anticipate. Uriah refused to go to his house to be
with his wife (11:9). Instead, he stayed in the guard
chamber of the palace with David's personal guard.
(The guard chamber is spoken about in I Kings 14:27-
28.) When the king found out the next morning what
had happened, he came to Uriah to determine why
(11:10). Uriah's reply must have made David feel very

small. Uriah would not enjoy the comforts of home and
the pleasures of his wife while Israel was at war. Uriah
felt that he belonged on the battleground—not the
playground (11:11).

In desperation David tried one more ploy. He told
Uriah to remain in Jerusalem one more day (11:12).
Rather than force Uriah to go home to enjoy a feast,
David had a banquet in the palace. David was determined to make Uriah drunk. In that condition he would
certainly forget his principles and stagger home to his
wife (11:13). Again David was frustrated, for Uriah had
more convictions in his stupor than David was evidenc-
ing in his sobriety.

An Unbelievable Message (11:14-17)

It was a sleepless night for the ruler of Israel. His
attempts to cover up his sin had been unsuccessful.
Frantically, he searched for an answer to his predicament. Seeing no other alternative, David sat down with
paper and pen as he had done so often in his life. It was
not a psalm that flowed from a joyful heart but rather a
sentence of death from a desperate king. In essence the
note said, "Send Uriah into the worst part of the fighting; then pull the rest of the troops back. Leave him
there to die" (paraphrase of 11:15). To make matters
worse, Uriah unknowingly carried his own death notice
to Joab (11:14).

Joab was a military man, pure and simple. He was
programmed to carry out orders without question. He
read the decree and ordered Uriah into the combat
where the best Ammonite fighters were engaged
(11:16). The fighting was fierce and many men died—
including a mighty man named Uriah (11:17).

An Unaffected Monarch (11:18-27)

Casualties on the Israeli side must have been excessively high because Joab feared that David might become angry when he learned of the death toll (11:19-20). The king might wonder why they had approached so closely to the city wall, knowing that the archers could inflict heavy losses on them (11:20). Perhaps David would cite an illustration from Israel's history where Abimelech was critically wounded at Thebez when a woman struck him with a millstone (cf. Judges 9:50-54). Under such questioning, the messenger was to inform the king that Uriah had died (11:21). Hopefully this would pacify the king.

The nervous messenger returned to Jerusalem and explained the outcome of the recent conflicts. The courier was so upset that he spoke of Uriah's death even before the king asked (11:23-24). David's response is another shocking development in a chain of startling actions: *"Let not this thing displease thee, for the sword devoureth one as well as another" (11:25).* In essence David was saying, "Tell Joab, 'You win some and you lose some.' " Look how far David's sin had carried him. He began with covetousness, tried to cover up, forced himself into further crime, and ended with callousness. Some of his most loyal men, who had stood by his side since the days of Saul, had been killed. Yet the king was unmoved through the hardness of his own sin. Relieved of the pressures of guilt, David issued a command for Joab to destroy Rabbah quickly.

When Bathsheba heard of her husband's death, she mourned, probably for seven days (cf. Genesis 50:10; I Samuel 31:13). No doubt this was genuine sorrow over her loss (11:26). After the period of mourning, David "legitimately" took Bathsheba as his wife (11:27). Everyone would look upon this as a kind gesture by a benevolent king. With a sigh of relief, David thought that everyone had been fooled. And this might have been so if God had not taken notice: *"But the thing that David had done displeased the Lord"* (11:27). The word *"displeased"* is the same word that occurs in verse twenty-five. It means "to be evil or bad." Joab was told not to view David's actions as being bad or evil, but God viewed them that way. David's basic problem was that he did not see his sin as God saw it.

Three principles emerge from the text. First, failure to perform in areas where we are responsible leaves us in a position where we are vulnerable. Had David been on the battlefield, he would never have confronted this more devastating enemy. Second, no one is ever immune to the temptations of sin. David was *"a man after God's own heart,"* but he still succumbed. David had enjoyed great success, but that did not keep him from failure. David was now over fifty years old, but the lust of the flesh was still strong. Third, failure to confess our sin will always result in serious consequences. David's seed of sin bore fruit in more sin, but the bitter harvest only begins with the catastrophe of the twelfth chapter.

Let's be honest. Collecting skeletons is not a viable hobby for the Christian.

TIMELESS TRUTHS FOR TODAY

---

1. **Failure to perform in areas where we are responsible leaves us in a position where we are vulnerable.**

2. **No one is ever immune to the temptations of sin.**

3. **Failure to confess our sin will always result in serious consequences.**

Chapter 13

What to Do When You Fail

II Samuel 12:1-31

Benjamin Franklin once stated, "How few there are who have courage enough to own their faults, or resolution enough to mend them!" An applicable illustration of that truth is reported in the first book of Samuel. Israel's first king, Saul, had been issued a divine command but had failed to obey (I Samuel 15:3, 9). When confronted by the prophet of God with his failures, Saul refused to admit guilt (I Samuel 15:13, 15, 20). After continued reproof, the king finally confessed, *"I have sinned,"* but tempered his confession with an excuse (I Samuel 15:24). Empty words! Because of his improper response concerning his sin, Saul's kingdom was ultimately destroyed.

Over a third of a century passed, and the moment of truth arrived for Israel's second king, David. He played the fool in allowing himself to indulge in his own lust. In a futile attempt to conceal his guilt, David had Uriah,

Bathsheba's husband, killed. It appeared that no one would ever know what really happened. Yet there will always be a day of reckoning. David's time had come. How he would respond was critical. Again, God sent His prophet to rebuke and restore His servant.

Guilt Exposed (12:1-12)

The most miserable people on earth are those who have experienced failure and have not risen above it. For nearly a year David was permitted to live in the anguish of his own guilt. In a sequel to Psalm 51, David reflected on his afflicted state: *"When I kept silence, my bones waxed old through my roaring all the day long. For day and night thy hand was heavy upon me: my moisture is turned into the drought of summer" (Psalm 32:3-4).* As a result of not confessing his sins, David was affected physically in the sapping of his energy and emotionally by his roaring ("groaning"). Sleep escaped him. Life became barren. He felt the heavy hand of God's chastisement upon him (cf. I Samuel 5:6).

At last Nathan was sent to confront the king. However, instead of direct condemnation, a folksy parable was used to disarm David from any attempt at self-justification. The story told by Nathan is one that related well to David, a former shepherd.

Two men lived in a city. One was rich, the other poor. The rich man owned much livestock. The poor man could hardly make ends meet, but he did own one little pet lamb (12:3), which he had bought and managed to keep alive. As is often the case, the little creature became part of the family, even eating and drinking from its master's plate and cup. One day a stranger came by the tents of the rich man (12:4). Custom dictates that the traveler should be fed and lodged. The rich man, being selfish by nature, took pity on his own possessions but was calloused toward the possessions of others. Having seized the poor man's lamb, he had it slaughtered and prepared for the wayfarer.

Perhaps David had seen similar instances take place during his shepherding years. The thought of a rich man stealing a poor man's pet lamb incensed the king (12:5). His judgment was that the man deserved to die and that he must *"restore the lamb fourfold" (12:6).* This restoration of property was in accordance with Mosaic Law (Exodus 22:1; cf. Luke 19:8).

Sentence had been passed. Nathan turned to the king and applied the parable, *"Thou art the man" (12:7).* The words cut quickly and deeply into the sleeping conscience of David. He was the *"rich man"* with his harem who had stolen the only wife of one of his loyal servants. Continuing his rebuke, Nathan shamed David by reminding him of God's blessings in four simple statements: *"I anointed thee . . . I delivered thee . . . I gave thee . . . I would moreover have given unto thee" (12:7-8).* Implied in the four expressions is the gift of God's power (authority), protection, provision, and promise. The last statement reveals that David could have had almost anything he wanted within the bounds of God's commands.

David's basic problem is mentioned in verse nine, *"Wherefore hast thou despised the commandment of the Lord, to do evil in his sight?"* The word *"despise"* means "to regard a thing as of little value, to treat lightly." The same Hebrew word is used of Esau's attitude toward his birthright (Genesis 25:34). David had taken a light view of God's command in committing adultery and murder. Inevitably his view of God's Word also meant a light view of God Himself (12:10).

The effects of David's sin would be bloodshed in his own house (12:10), rebellion from among his children

(12:11), and sexual defilement within his own family (12:11-12). These judgments would be public since David was in leadership and bore greater responsibility, accompanied by greater accountability. A final penalty was pronounced after David's repentance. David's heart must have ached when he learned that the child born from the unholy union would die (12:14).

Grief Expressed (12:13-19; cf. Psalms 32 and 51)

Facing his guilt honestly and openly, David confessed that he had sinned (12:13). After this Nathan guaranteed the king that he would not die as prescribed in the law (Leviticus 20:10; 24:17). A fuller expression of David's repentance and attitudes is preserved in his great penitential psalm (Psalm 51). David's confession produced forgiveness (I John 1:9). However, since David's actions had caused God to be disrespected by Israel's enemies, God had to demonstrate His displeasure by taking the life of the child born to the king and Bathsheba (12:14). When Nathan left, the child was *"struck"* with sickness (12:15). The word for *"struck"* is almost always used of divine judgment, and its noun form means "plague" (e.g., the plagues of Egypt). The child was said to be *"very sick."* The idea conveyed in the Hebrew is that of an incurable sickness (Jeremiah 15:18; 30:12). Interestingly, this word is used of our heart's spiritual condition (Jeremiah 17:9).

Hoping that God might allow the child to live, David prayed for mercy (12:16). His earnestness is evidenced in his fasting and humility. Even when his chief advisors tried to console him and urged him to take food, he would not (12:17). Seven days later the child died, but the servants hesitated to tell the mourning king for fear he would harm (KJV *"vex"*) himself (12:18). While they whispered, David saw them and reasoned that the child had died. After asking them straightforwardly about the matter, the death was verified (12:19).

Grace Experienced (12:20-31)

Rather than "falling to pieces," David showed remarkable calm upon hearing the dreadful news. First, he arose from the earth, washed himself, and used fragrant oils on his body. Then he changed into some fresh clothes and went to the house of God to worship (12:20). *"Worship"* here means to prostrate oneself in submission. He was symbolically yielding to God's will. Finally, he returned home where he asked for food and sat down to eat. Shocked by David's reactions, the servants inquired, *"What thing is this that thou hast done?"* (12:21). David fasted and wept for his living child but now arose and ate *"after the death"* of his child. Such a backward response did not make sense to them. The king's answer to his people is a beautiful picture of the three keys to handling life's problems.

David explained that he had fasted and wept for the sick child, hoping that God might be gracious and allow the child to live. When the child died, there was nothing more that could be done. This then is the first key: "You can't change the past" (12:23a). The second key to handling life's problems is seen in David's actions in verse twenty. When there was no more hope for the child, David realized that life had to go on. Stated another way, "You must live one day at a time in the present." The concluding words of this monarch have been a comfort to many families who have lost young children in death. *"I shall go to him, but he shall not return to me"* (12:23b). The implication is that young children who die are given eternal life by God's grace. David fully expected to see his child again. This statement, along with the example of David's worship (12:20), reveals the third key to handling problems: "You must trust God for the future." The only explanation for David's composure at this troublesome time was that he was experiencing God's matchless grace.

Verses twenty-four and twenty-five obviously take place in a time frame later than the other events of the chapter. These events are recorded here in order to finish the story and further demonstrate grace. Although nothing is said of Bathsheba's emotions during the child's sickness and death, we can be assured that she had gone through intense suffering. As was fitting, David comforted his wife. The tears were turned to joy as God blessed them with a son whom they named Solomon ("peaceable"). God Himself had a special love for that child. For the second time in this chapter, Nathan was sent to the palace. This time he bore words of encouragement. God had given Solomon a second name, Jedidiah. The name *"Jedidiah,"* which means "beloved of the Lord," declared that the sin of this couple was in the past, and the future looked bright.

The Lord further encouraged David by a decisive victory over the Ammonites. War at Rabbah had continued for a year or more. This lingering problem might have been God's way of seeking to humble David. But after David's confession of sin, miraculously Joab was able to inflict devastating blows, and victory was imminent (12:26-27). Joab called for David to bring troops and lead the final battle lest he (Joab) should take the city, and it be called after Joab's name (12:28). Joab's humility is remarkable for a man in his position.

In accordance with Joab's wishes, David assembled his men and came to Rabbah (12:29). Victory came quickly with David taking a great abundance of spoil,

including the king's crown of gold and precious jewels
(12:30), which weighed approximately ninety-two
pounds. The prisoners of war (probably the soldiers)
were executed by means of saws, harrows, axes of iron,
and incineration in brick-kilns (12:31; cf. I Chronicles
20:3). The harrows were sharp iron instruments used
as threshing sledges. These extremely torturous deaths
might have been implemented because of the brutality
of the Ammonites (I Samuel 11:2; Amos 1:13).

From the narratives of the twelfth chapter we learn
three important lessons. First, it is easier to point a finger than to admit our failures. For nearly a year David
lived with his own guilt, unwilling to humble himself
and confess it. But when he saw a similar transgression
through Nathan's parable, he was quick to condemn.
Second, failure is not the end; it's the beginning. The
exposure of sin did not destroy the king. Instead, it
motivated him to renew his relationship with God and
begin a new chapter in his life (Proverbs 24:16). Third,
where sin abounds, grace can much more abound (Romans 5:20). David could have easily thought that God
had given up on him and that His blessing would be
removed. Yet God graciously withheld His hand of
judgment on David himself (12:13), placed His blessing
on a succeeding child (12:24-25), and provided victory
over David's enemies (12:29-30).

Have you met with failure in your life? Do you feel
as if you are all washed up? Take courage from David, a
man who failed but was not a failure, because he for-
sook his sin.

TIMELESS TRUTHS FOR TODAY

How to Handle Your Failures and Problems:

1. You can't change the past.

2. You must live one day at a time in the present.

3. You must trust God for the future.

Additional Principles:

1. It is easier to point a finger than to admit our failures.

2. Failure is not the end; it's the beginning.

3. Where sin abounds, grace can much more abound.

Chapter 14

The Harvest Begins
II Samuel 13:1-22

We are living in the computer age, or so we are told! But did you know that computers of one form or another have been around for nearly five thousand years? The Babylonians were the first to develop a primitive computer for making mathematical calculations. We remember this calculator as an abacus. Computers have come a long way since then. In 1833 an Englishman by the name of Charles Babbage assembled the first automatic calculating machine. Its functions included determining logarithms and plotting lunar positions. However, it took a world war (the second) to accelerate computer study and production into the modern age. Data was needed to calculate the trajectory of shells.

The first commercial computer was used in 1951 and helped record the United States census. Shortly thereafter a company by the name of International Business

Machines (IBM) began selling computers commercially. Today the market is flooded with computers of varying abilities and prices, including computers for home use. One of the most fascinating computers known weighs only three pounds. Using billions of microcomponents, it is capable of generating the power to transmit signals across millions of interconnections in a split second. In fact, this computer can daily use one hundred times more connections than the telephone systems of the entire world. The ability to program this device is phenomenal. Depending on the speed of the programmer, this computer can receive ten new items of information per second during its entire lifetime. Although it is readily available to the general public, few have availed themselves of its potential. Unfortunately, many of those who have taken advantage of this resource have misused it. By the way, this computer does not have a trade name. We call it the human brain.

II Samuel 13 preserves the story of a young man who failed to program his God-given "computer" properly. Feeding his lust continuously with impure thoughts, this young man let his passions finally break loose, and he committed a violent act against an innocent girl. The details of the story are repulsive. The pleas of the young maiden are heartrending. Still, God allowed this incident to be inscribed in His Word to teach us important truths about dealing with lust and the consequences if we fail to do so.

The Infatuation with a Fair Sister (13:1-2)

David's eldest son was born in Hebron (II Samuel 3:2). His name was Amnon, meaning "faithful." Without a doubt, the king had great plans for his little boy. Since Amnon was the firstborn, he was heir to the throne. As he grew he watched his father closely and patterned his life after his hero, King David. It is only fitting that a child should walk in his father's footsteps, but David's footprints marked a path leading to the miry pit of moral impurity. Amnon had seen his father take another man's wife, endeavor to cover up his guilt, and nearly get away with it.

The older Amnon grew, the greater his moral battles became. Like his father, he had a weakness for sensual pleasures. This weakness was nurtured through an uncontrolled thought life. Possibly during one of the court feasts he had spied a beautiful young girl by the name of Tamar. Although her age is not given, she was probably in her early teen years. Tamar was the sister of Absalom, the third of David's sons born in Hebron. Her mother was a foreign princess from Geshur. David's being the father of both Amnon and Tamar made them related as half brother and half sister. The Bible describes the girl as *"fair."* The Hebrew behind this word means "to be beautiful in outward appearance." Obviously, good looks ran in the family, for the same word is used of David (I Samuel 17:42) and Absalom (II Samuel 14:25).

Amnon fell in love with his sister, but she was off limits to him. Mosaic Law had clearly stated that marriage and marital relations were forbidden in this case (Leviticus 18:9, 11). Any such violation is strongly denounced as *"wicked"* (Leviticus 20:17). But Amnon could not keep his mind off beautiful Tamar. Of Amnon it is reported that he was *"so vexed, that he fell sick for his sister"* (13:2). Here *"to vex"* literally means "to bind," and it portrays the idea of being tied up in knots emotionally. This sexual frustration created a psychosomatic disorder in Amnon. When the passage states that *"he fell sick,"* it should be translated "he made (caused) himself to be sick." But *"Amnon thought it hard for him to do anything to her" (13:2)*. The understanding of this phrase is cleared up in the definition of *"thought it hard."* This word is often used of God's marvelous, miraculous works among men. When it is used of men, however, it speaks of activities which are beyond normal human capabilities. Since Tamar was a virgin, his half sister, and under the protection of her mother's harem, Amnon thought it impossible to fulfill his inordinate desires.

The Influence of a Friend (13:3-5)

At this critical moment a new character is introduced. Jonadab is labeled as Amnon's friend (13:3). Although this is a normal word for friend, it can be used with tongue in cheek since this same word is used of Job's three friends. Incidentally, this is not the word used of David and Jonathan's friendship. Jonadab is described as a *"subtil"* (literally "wise") man. His wisdom was worldly wisdom. In the New Testament James says of this wisdom that it is *"earthly, sensual, devilish" (James 3:15)*. It accomplishes selfish goals with total disregard for the feelings or damage done to others.

Apparently, Amnon and Jonadab were accustomed to spending time together. Implied in the text is a daily meeting between the two, usually in the morning (13:4). Jonadab had begun to notice a change in Amnon's appearance. He seemed low or depressed (KJV *"lean"*) morning after morning. This may have been due to his struggles with immoral thoughts throughout the night. When asked what troubled him, Amnon responded, *"I love Tamar, my brother Absalom's sister" (13:4)*. He did not say, "Tamar, my sister." That would have admitted greater guilt. Slyly he was justifying the entertainment of his evil thoughts.

Rather than being a true friend, Jonadab devised a wicked plot by which Amnon could defile his sister. Amnon was to lie down upon his bed, pretending to be sick (13:5). When David visited his invalid son, Amnon was to request Tamar to come and cook privately for him.

The Incest by Force (13:6-17)

The temptation is for us to read so "matter-of-factly" the details of what takes place. Bear in mind the emotions that come into play. The story comes alive as one senses the terror of Tamar and the hardness of Amnon.

According to plan, Amnon feigned sickness and was visited by his father (13:6). When Tamar was requested personally to attend to Amnon, David fulfilled the wish (13:7). Soon a beautiful young lass stood before her brother and began to prepare a special heart-shaped bread (13:8). Upon finishing her cooking, three unusual events transpired that should have warned Tamar of impending trouble. First, Amnon refused to eat what he had requested (13:9). Second, he removed all the servants from the room (13:9). Third, he retired to the bedroom *("chamber")*, ordering Tamar to bring the food to him there.

In Tamar's defense we must observe that she was naive, being young and sheltered from wicked influences. Her dress was modest (cf. 13:18), and she had given no indication of being "loose." Innocently, she walked into the bedroom with the bread. Amnon forcibly grabbed her and in vile terms invited his sister to commit incest with him.

Shocked by the circumstances, Tamar quickly tried to reason with her abductor, *"Nay, my brother, do not force me; for no such thing ought to be done in Israel" (13:12).* To her credit she refused, identifying such force as not true love, and appealing to the testimony of Israel and ultimately of God as reason for not cooperating. She further sought to stir Amnon's conscience by pointing out the grave results this would have on both of their lives (13:13). Tamar must have sensed that Amnon was not listening, and she grasped at one last straw, *"Speak unto the king; for he will not withhold me from thee."* But Amnon knew the law. It was not possible for him to marry his half sister. Besides, lust is not interested in marriage, only self-gratification.

Amnon, being stronger than the young girl, forced her to his bed. Terror, pain, and tears were experienced for what must have seemed like an eternity. Within minutes the ordeal, in one sense, was over (13:14). Amnon's lust was fulfilled, but it brought no satisfaction. His insensitivity is evident in that his love (really lust) turned to hatred, and with bitterness he ordered, "Get up and get out" (13:15).

Tamar refused to leave, knowing that she would be branded a prostitute and declared to be the guilty party (13:16). Amnon then called one of his servants, who was directed to throw Tamar out and bolt the door. Again his callousness is obvious as he does not even use her name. He refers to her as *"this woman" (13:17).*

The Impact on the Family (13:18-22)

Tamar was a devastated woman. She had nowhere to turn; her future was destroyed. She expressed her helpless, mournful state by putting ashes on her head, tearing her beautiful princess robe, and throwing her face in her hands as she wept uncontrollably (13:19). The Hebrew word for *"cry"* was normally used of crying out to God in time of distress (cf. Judges 6:6-7).

When she returned home, Absalom suspected what had taken place and tried to calm his sister as much as possible. She was to remain in Absalom's house the rest of her life, desolate (13:20). *"Desolate"* does not mean without a husband, but conveys the thought of emotional devastation. I wonder if she ever mentally and emotionally recovered from this episode. From that day forward Absalom would not speak to his brother, and he developed a deep hatred against Amnon (13:22).

David's reaction to the crime should have been immediate. Amnon's sin called for capital punishment (Leviticus 20:17). The writer records that David was *"very wroth"* (literally "burned") and nothing more. No action was taken against the offender. Perhaps he saw a glimpse of himself and his own weaknesses that were now reproduced in his son. Seeds had been sown. The harvest had begun.

This is a story we would rather forget. Yet similar events are enacted day after day in our society because lust still exists. In applying what we have witnessed in this chapter, let's observe five truths about lust.

1. Thinking of lust leads to activity. Because Amnon failed to control his thoughts, they controlled him.

2. Reasoning with lust leads to futility. Tamar tried her best to reason her way out of the problem. However, God did not command us to reason with moral impurity; He commanded us to flee (II Timothy 2:22).

3. Indulging in lust leads to animosity. Amnon's "love" quickly turned to hate when he had satisfied his desires. And his hatred was evident in his coarse words to Tamar thereafter.

4. Participating in lust leads to despondency. The guilt of sexual sin is difficult to escape. Tamar experienced emotional devastation the rest of her life.

5. Abstaining from lust leads to purity. A war is being waged against the purity of young lives (I Peter 2:11).

The way of victory is founded on Biblical convictions and firm resolution to abstain from lust. If you are fighting some battles along this "front," remember the scars of Tamar. Hers never healed—and neither will yours.

TIMELESS TRUTHS FOR TODAY

---

1. Uncontrolled lust will always seek to control you.

2. Ungodly friends will always seek to influence you.

3. Unchaste behavior will always seek to destroy you.

Chapter 15

Bitter-Sweet Revenge
II Samuel 13:23-39

Does the name Morgan Robertson mean anything to you? Perhaps not. He was an English novelist who lived from 1861 to 1915. Among his many adventures written about the sea is an interesting one published in 1898 under the title *Futility*. The story revolves around the maiden voyage of a British luxury liner, the *Titan*. The ship sailed from Southampton bound for America, loaded with affluent passengers celebrating the launching of the grandest oceanliner ever built and considered to be "unsinkable." But *Titan* never reached her destination. An iceberg floating in the icy North Atlantic waters ripped a hole in the hull of the ship. The ship sank and many lives were lost. Of course, that was only fiction.

Fourteen years later another ship left harbor at Southampton on her maiden voyage. Many dignitaries and families of great wealth were booked on this initial cruise, which was to be a gala event. Great publicity surrounded this liner since if was then the largest and the most magnificent ship to sail the oceans to date. The liner had been specially constructed with a double-bottomed hull, which contained sixteen watertight compartments. Any four of these compartments could suffer damage and be flooded without affecting the buoyancy of the ship. Because of its unique construction, this ship, the *Titanic*, was labeled "unsinkable." But on the night of April 14, 1912, while cruising along at a careless twenty-two knots in the dangerous North Atlantic, a sudden jolt alarmed the crew and the passengers. A mammoth iceberg had torn a three-hundred-foot gash in the side of the ship, flooding five compartments. The liner was ill-equipped for this emergency. The capacity of the lifeboats was not enough for the number of passengers aboard, and hope of survival in the cold Atlantic waters was futile. The ship sank within two hours and forty minutes. The death toll stood at 1513. What had started out as a grand celebration ended as a grisly catastrophe.

The account before us also begins as a celebration but ends as a catastrophe. Winter had passed; the new year had begun. It was sheepshearing time, and excitement filled the air as anticipation mounted concerning the accompanying festivities. The celebrations would soon be under way, but the party would be tragically disrupted by a savage murder.

The Request of Absalom (13:23-27)

"And it came to pass after two full years" (13:23). This verse refers to the events recorded earlier in the chapter. Absalom's sister Tamar had been forcibly raped by her half brother Amnon (13:14). Because of this vile act,

Absalom had developed a deep resentment against
Amnon and refused to speak to him (13:22). For two
long years that bitterness had eaten away on Absalom's
spirit. Thoughts of "getting even" had crossed his mind
many times; however, no suitable opportunity had
presented itself.

Now Absalom came before the king to make a request. Initially, it seems there were no thoughts of malice or revenge. The feasts associated with sheepshearing were near. Absalom's sheep were being sheared
near the border of Ephraim in the village of Baal-hazor
approximately fourteen miles northeast of Jerusalem
(13:23). In preparation for the big event, Absalom was
hurriedly extending invitations to all the king's sons.
How prestigious if David himself would attend! So
Absalom asked his father and his servants to honor him
with a royal visit (13:24).

David attempted to excuse himself by saying, *"Nay,
my son, let us not all now go, lest we be chargeable unto thee"*
(13:25). *"Chargeable"* means "to be heavy or burden-
some." The presence of the king's court might be too
great a burden on Absalom and his attendants. Absalom
refused to be rejected so easily. Great preparation and
planning had been made. Besides, Absalom might have
felt his reputation as one of the king's sons was at
stake. Therefore, Absalom *"pressed"* his father to go.
This word for *"press"* is used of the pressure exerted
upon an immovable object such as a wall, with the result
that there is a breakthrough. Even after the pressure,
David stood firm, and the real reason is revealed. *"How-
beit he would not go" (13:25).* Literally, the Hebrew says,
"And he was not willing to go." David just did not want
to take the time to participate in the interests of his
son. This possibly strikes a responsive chord in the
hearts of many fathers who are too busy to take an

interest in the activities of their children. Such insensitivity can produce an unwanted reaction. Paul warned, *"Fathers, provoke not your children to anger, lest they be discouraged" (Colossians 3:21)*. Fathers, we can quickly cause our children to be disheartened by uncalled-for irritation. David's response to Absalom must have broken his spirit. Then to add insult to injury, David *"blessed"* his son, which would be like saying, "Have a great party!" How can you have a great party without the king?

Not willing to leave entirely empty-handed, Absalom made a slight change in his request. This may be the point where Absalom decided to avenge his sister's shame. He asked if Amnon, as David's representative, might be permitted to attend the celebration. The king was curious as to why Amnon should go (13:26), but Absalom's answer is not given. However, he did continue to pressure his father until, in desperation, David yielded to the request and even decided to send all his sons (13:27). (Although it is impossible to prove beyond doubt, David might have thought Absalom would not harm Amnon while in the company of all the king's sons.) From this incident and what follows, we should learn that hasty decisions made under pressure can lead to disaster.

The Revenge Against Amnon (13:28-29)

Absalom seized the opportunity before him. Meeting privately with his servants in hushed tones, he ordered them to keep a careful watch over Amnon. When it was evident that Amnon was oblivious to his surroundings, Absalom would issue a command to kill Amnon (13:28). Their faces must have registered surprise and fear, for Absalom said, *"Fear not: have not I commanded you?"* This statement was made not only to dispel any doubt but

also to assure them that Absalom assumed full responsibility for the deed. Then Absalom said something
rather ironic, *"Be courageous, be valiant."* These were words
normally associated with acts of highest character. Bitterness had so clouded Absalom's judgment that he
called evil *good*.

Finally, the fateful day arrived. Absalom and Amnon
were seated in the most prominent places surrounded
by the other sons of the king. Music filled the air, food
was abundant, and wine flowed freely. Everyone was
caught up in the merriment of the moment—everyone
except Absalom, who scanned the scene with watching
eye, waiting to vent his anger on his unsuspecting
brother. Then the hour came; the command was
shouted. Instantly, Amnon was engulfed by his enemies. When the servants had finished their brutal act,
Amnon lay in a pool of blood.

The remaining participants fled in horror. Jumping
on their mules, they ran for their lives. (I can't help
wondering if one of those mules decided to be stubborn
at that inopportune time and threw his would-be rider
into near panic.)

The Remorse at Jerusalem (13:30-36)

While the king's sons were in transit to Jerusalem,
word came to the king of what had taken place. The
report contained the rumor that all the king's sons had
been killed (13:30). David, believing the news, tore his
clothes and fell on his face in mourning, as did all of his
servants (13:31). David's nephew, Jonadab, stepped
forward to comfort the king.

Jonadab believed that only Amnon had been slain in
Baal-hazor. His reasoning was clear. He had heard statements from Absalom's lips concerning his intentions.

And it was Amnon only who had defiled Tamar (13:32).

Soon the guard in the watchtower spied a pack of fast-moving mules carrying the king's sons approaching from the west side of Jerusalem (13:34). It was evident that Jonadab's words were true. Smugly he remarked, "I told you so." (Cf. 13:35.) Jonadab was a young man who manipulated others to gain advantage for himself. Apparently, he knew in advance what would happen in Baal-hazor; but he did not tell his "friend" Amnon of the danger. Nor did he try to stop Absalom. Absalom was now the heir apparent and could promote a confidant like Jonadab. Jonadab's words of "comfort" to David would insure friendly relations with the throne. When he ceased speaking, the sons of David entered their father's presence and all wept over the tragedy that had occurred (13:36).

The Retreat Across the Jordan (13:37-39)

Absalom knew the gravity of the situation and resolved to hide until things cooled off. Since logically he could not remain within reach of his father, he fled to Talmai, King of Geshur, who was his grandfather (13:37; cf. 3:3). Absalom's self-imposed exile extended over three years (13:38). During that time David mourned daily over the loss of his firstborn, Amnon (13:37).

Verse thirty-nine reads, *"And the soul of King David longed to go forth unto Absalom."* This implies that all was forgiven and that David wanted to mend his relationship with Absalom. However, the context of this statement, with the event of the following chapter, lends credibility to an alternate translation. "And this [Absalom's residence with Talmai] restrained King David from going forth against Absalom." In other words, at the time of Amnon's death, David was prepared to punish Absalom for his crime. As months passed, however, David's grief began to wane for his dead son.

A common thread—bitterness—weaves its way through Absalom's life. In this and succeeding chapters, we will observe the terrible cost of having a bitter spirit. The story of Absalom's revenge against Amnon exhibits several truths. First, bitterness robs us of our joy. When everyone else was enjoying the party, Absalom was filled with malice. Second, bitterness clouds our minds in making good judgments. Absalom believed the murder of Amnon would be a valiant act (13:28). Third, bitterness cannot be hidden from others. Jonadab had heard Absalom's venomous words on previous occasions (13:32). Fourth, bitterness often leads to revenge. And fifth, bitterness brings about broken fellowship. Absalom was separated from his friends and from his father. No wonder the writer of Hebrews wrote, *"Looking diligently lest any man fail of the grace of God, lest any root of bitterness springing up trouble you, and thereby many be defiled" (Hebrews 12:15).*

TIMELESS TRUTHS FOR TODAY

The Effects of Bitterness:

1. Bitterness robs you of your joy.

2. Bitterness keeps you from making good judgments.

3. Bitterness cannot be hidden from others.

4. Bitterness often leads to revenge.

5. Bitterness results in broken fellowship.

Chapter 16

I Forgive You, But . . .
II Samuel 14:1-33

The following allegory is attributed to Aesop, the famed fabulist of the sixth century B.C. "A country-man's son by accident trod upon a serpent's tail, which turned and bit him so that he died. The father in a rage got his axe, and pursuing the serpent, cut off part of its tail. So the serpent in revenge began stinging several of the farmer's cattle and caused him severe loss. Well, the farmer thought it best to make it up with the serpent, and brought food and honey to the mouth of its lair, and said to it: 'Let's forget and forgive; perhaps you were right to punish my son, and take vengeance on my cattle, but surely I was right in trying to revenge him; now that we are both satisifed, why should not we be friends again?'

'No, no,' said the serpent; 'take away your gifts; you can never forget the death of your son, nor I the loss of my tail.' "

Substitute the names David and Absalom in the place of farmer and serpent. Rewritten this way, Aesop could have submitted the story to *Reader's Digest* as a "condensed" version of II Samuel 13 and 14. Absalom had murdered David's firstborn son, Amnon, in an act of revenge over the sexual crime committed against Tamar (II Samuel 13). For fear of punishment, Absalom fled to the safety of his grandparents' home in Geshur, where he hid for three years. Meanwhile, David mourned the loss of his son but failed to execute justice in the matter, just as he had neglected to do in Amnon's case. Certainly David's previous sins of immorality and murder had robbed him of the character and courage to act decisively at these critical moments. Cleverly, Joab devised a plan to force David to allow Absalom to return home. Unfortunately, David forgave without forgetting, and Absalom returned without repenting.

Joab's Fabrication (14:1-11)

During Absalom's three-year absence, Joab may have tried and failed on several occasions to have the exiled son restored, as implied in verses nineteen and twenty-two. Although verse one states that *"the king's heart was toward Absalom,"* a better translation would be, "the king's heart was against Absalom." There are three reasons for adopting this alternative. First, the Hebrew word translated *"toward"* (*'al*) is commonly translated "against." (Cf. II Samuel 11:23; 12:11; 14:7, 13; etc.) In the only other instance where a similar syntax occurs, the preposition is clearly translated *"against"* (*Daniel 11:28*). The extended context of this narration does have a reference to the hearts of men being toward Absalom in a good sense, but the Hebrew word is entirely different (15:13). The second reason for believing David was continuing to withstand Absalom is suggested in the necessity of using the entrapping tale of verses six and seven. The final argument for David's enmity with his son is his refusal to permit Absalom to enter the palace (14:24, 28). If David's heart longed for the return of his son, why did he deny Absalom the privilege of facing him? The sting of Amnon's death had not worn off.

Since Absalom was now heir apparent to the throne, Joab might have reasoned that political expediency demanded that Absalom return to Israel. Absence of the heir could prove disastrous if David were to die suddenly. (Many commentators believe David suffered great physical disorders during Absalom's banishment.) Joab could also insure a favorable reception for himself under the next monarch by securing a safe return for Absalom.

The most effective way of accomplishing his purposes was to use a fanciful story vaguely paralleling what had taken place in the kingdom and then applying it to the present circumstance. Joab had seen Nathan use this same tactic with great success (12:1-7). Enlisting the services of a wise woman of Tekoah, a town midway between Jerusalem and Hebron, Joab ordered her to pretend (KJV *"feign"*) to be a mourner for a dead son (14:2). She was then given the words to speak before the king (14:3).

After rehearsing her "lines," she approached David to ask for mercy (14:4). David acknowledged her and the charade began. Claiming to be a widow, she informed the king that her two sons had been fighting in the field. No one tried to separate them, and ultimately one son was killed (14:6). The death stirred up the whole family with the result that they wanted to avenge the slain son by the blood of the other son

(14:7). Playing on the sentiments of the listening monarch, she emphasized that the living son was the heir and also the last *"coal"* of her *"fire."* Without him the family name would die (14:7).

For some unknown reason David attempted to delay judgment (14:8). In spite of that, the woman urged David on by assuming responsibility and any corresponding guilt that a favorable verdict might bring (14:9). Yielding to the pretender's plea, David assured the woman of protection from her oppressors (14:10). But this was not enough. When she asked David to make an oath that her son would go unharmed, he complied (14:11). Precedent was therefore established for similar judgments.

The Parable's Application (14:12-17)

Having received permission to continue her audience with the king (14:12), the woman frankly applied the story. In essence she said, "Why don't you practice what you preach?" (14:13). Accusing him of inconsistency, she caught David off guard. Then with some homespun, half-baked theology, she reasoned with the king that everyone must die and any deeds done could not then be undone. If David wanted to undo the past, he must take action at once. A spiritual note is added that even God devises ways of restoring those who are banished from His fellowship. While on the surface this appears true, it is not the whole truth. God's mercy in restoring those who have wandered from Him is predicated not upon sentimentality but upon judicial activity. Penalties must be paid; restitution must be made. Although God is love, He is also a holy, just God. These are balancing truths of theology. The exclusion of love leads to coarse insensitivity. The exclusion of justice leads to shallow sentimentality. This latter imbalanced theology swayed David.

Seeking to absolve herself of any possible reproof from the king, she revealed that others had forced her to make this appearance before him (14:15), reminded him of her alleged plight (14:16), and flattered him for his wisdom (14:17).

David's Declaration (14:18-24)

David could withhold his suspicions no longer, and he bluntly asked if Joab were behind this scheme (14:18, 19). Hidden away carefully in garnishes of praise to David was the admission of Joab's involvement (14:19-20).

Joab, ever near the king, was summoned to bring Absalom back to Jerusalem (14:21). Upon hearing these words, Joab bowed and thanked the king, saying, *"Today thy servant knoweth that I have found grace in thy sight, my lord, O king, in that the king hath fulfilled the request of his servant" (14:22)*. Concealed in that statement is the evidence of previous requests.

The declaration of Absalom's restoration included two stipulations (14:24). One, Absalom must return to his own house. (This might have been a restriction similar to those imposed on Adonijah and Shimei. See I Kings 1:53; 2:36.) Two, he would not be permitted to see the king's face. So Joab did as he was commanded and escorted Absalom from Geshur (14:23).

Absalom's Indignation (14:25-33)

The last nine verses of this chapter supply us with some insight as to the person and personality of Absalom. Previously we have observed that he was the third

130 Rubbing Elbows with Royalty

son born to David while in Hebron (3:3). His mother was a foreign princess from Geshur. Although his name means "father of peace," his actions betrayed his name. When he learned of Amnon's sin, he bore a grudge which led to murder (13:22, 28). Now something of his appearance is revealed (14:25). We are told that Absalom was extremely handsome, being void of any physical defect. His looks had the entire nation talking about this young man. He would have won all the popularity contests. In fact, his popularity was so widespread that he was voted "the most likely to secede." (Or is that *succeed?*) One additional note is made about his appearance. He took pride in his hair. Every year he got a "trim." When the cuttings were weighed, they amounted to two hundred shekels or approximately four and a half pounds (14:26).

Absalom was married. (I wonder what her hair looked like!) From that union were born three sons, who probably died in infancy since no names are recorded; and a daughter, whom he named Tamar after his sister (14:27). After this personal and family information the story continues.

For two long years Absalom remained in Jerusalem without seeing his father's face (14:28). Imagine the animosity this created in the son who was to sit on Israel's throne. Finally, unable to handle the rejection longer, he sent for Joab. When Joab failed to respond, Absalom called him a second time with still no answer (14:29). Absalom decided to take a drastic course of action. Joab happened to own property next door to Absalom. After assembling his servants, Absalom ordered them to set Joab's barley field on fire (14:30). When Joab saw what was happening, he came running and demanded, *"Wherefore have thy servants set my field on fire?"* To this Absalom responded, *"Behold, I sent unto thee saying, Come hither,"* (Or more commonly, "Look, when I say come, you come!") Absalom had a job for Joab. He wanted him to appeal to David concerning his restrictions to the palace. Under current conditions Absalom thought it senseless for him to have returned to Jerusalem. And if the king felt Absalom had sinned, Absalom brashly invited his father to kill him (14:32). Obediently Joab delivered the message to David. In what must have been a cool reception, Absalom haughtily entered the king's court, bowed mechanically, and received a kiss from his father, which restored him to his full privileges (14:33).

It is impossible to read this paragraph of Scripture without being aware of Absalom's pride. Several trademarks of pride are imprinted on his personality.

1. Pride delights in the flattery of others (14:25). The praise of people was music in Absalom's ears. He should have been far more concerned about what God thought of him rather than what men thought.

2. Pride disregards the rights of others (14:30, 32). Not only did Absalom expect Joab to hop when he said, "Jump," but he destroyed Joab's property to get his attention.

3. Pride denies wrongs done to others (14:32). Absalom stated, *"If there be any iniquity in me."* There was no way his pride would let him admit that he had been wrong.

4. Pride demands recognition from others (14:32). Absalom demanded an audience with the king and used Joab as a servant.

5. Pride displays false humility before others (14:33). Although Absalom bowed before the king, it was only his head and not his heart.

Looking back over this chapter, two problems are evident—David was not fully able to forgive his son Absalom; and Absalom, because of pride, was not willing to repent of his past sins. Failure to resolve both of these problems leads to the rebellion of chapter fifteen.

What can we learn from this failure? Two principles stand out in my mind. First, for forgiveness to be genuine, it must be total. Charles Spurgeon offered this advice—"Forgive and forget. When you bury a mad dog, don't leave his tail above the ground." The second lesson to be discovered is that for repentance to be genuine, it must be humble.

To put these principles into practice is tough, but so is the way of those who fail to live by them.

TIMELESS TRUTHS FOR TODAY

---

1. For forgiveness to be genuine, it must be total.

2. For repentance to be genuine, it must be humble.

Chapter 17

How to Spot
a Troublemaker

II Samuel 15:1-12

Wol was one of a pair of great horned owls that lived with a family residing in Saskatoon in the early 1930's. Normally a well-trained, well-behaved bird, he had made friends with the family dog, Mutt. The two owls and dog enjoyed weekend camping trips together, especially the ride in the rumble seat of the Model A roadster. However, Wol at times could be a trouble-maker. The object of his pranks was often Mutt. On lazy summer days Mutt would invariably walk over to Wol's favorite tree to satisfy himself that Wol was sleeping. Returning to his resting spot, Mutt would lie down and drift off into his afternoon snooze. Wol, who had only feigned his sleep, then cautiously crept up behind Mutt, staying close to the dog's rear. Ceremoni-ously he would raise his inch-long talons, gleefully stare at his unsuspecting victim, and proceed to pinch Mutt's tail. In near frenzy Mutt jumped and turned to find his tormenter. But Wol had escaped to the nearest tree, where he seemingly expressed his innocence with a vibrating question, "Whoo—whoo—whoo?"

We've all met troublemakers of one kind or another, but none match the mischief of David's third-born son, Absalom. Consumed by the bitterness of his father's rejection over a five-year period, Absalom turned in anger against his own flesh and blood. Wickedly he plotted a course that would emotionally devastate his father but ultimately lead to his own undoing. As we scan the scene of the first twelve verses of II Samuel 15, analyze carefully Absalom's actions. They reveal the marks of a traitor—the characteristics of a trouble-maker.

Undermining David's Power (15:1-6)

The chapter begins with the formula that calls to our attention what has preceded, *"And it came to pass after this" (15:1).* The reference is to the two years spent in Jerusalem during which Absalom had not been permitted to see David's face (14:24, 28). Although Absalom finally insisted on and forced a meeting, there was no forgiveness or repentance by either party. Absalom now determined to take matters into his own hands, undermine David's authority, and mastermind a plan which would establish Absalom on the throne. Absalom undermined the power of his father through impression (15:1), question (15:2-3), suggestion (15:4), and association with all the men of Israel (15:5-6).

One of the first courses Absalom took was the preparation of chariots, horses, and fifty men to run through the streets ahead of him. The spectacle would be similar to a parade honoring a hero. Such pomp often accompanied those who aspired to rule, as was the case with Adonijah a few years later (I Kings 1:5). Years before, Samuel prophesied that future kings would *"take your sons, and appoint them for himself, for his chariots, and to be his horsemen; and some shall run before his chariots"* (I Samuel 8:11). What a dramatic fulfillment Absalom's actions were! He was hoping to impress the people with his display of splendor and win them over to his cause.

Next Absalom sought to question the administrative ability of the king. Rising up early in the morning, he would wait by the street near the gate of the king's palace where men would come to present their lawsuits against others. The gate was the appointed place of judgment for legal matters (Deuteronomy 16:18; 21:19; 25:7; Proverbs 31:23). Here Absalom would be able to make friends with those who were disgruntled over unfavorable decisions. Absalom's approach was simple. Strike up a conversation (15:2b), listen to the complaints, and side with the complainer, saying, *"See, thy matters are good and right; but there is no man deputed of the king to hear thee"* (15:3). Because David had failed to appoint a "listener" to the problems, Absalom turned this into a springboard for his political plunge.

Commonly located near the gates were broad plazas where people could gather for marketing, meetings, or in this case, for rulings. Seizing his opportunity, Absalom proclaimed for all to hear, *"Oh that I were made judge in the land, that every man which hath any suit or cause might come unto me, and I would do him justice!"* (15:4). Literally he said, "Who will make me king?" This stirred considerable debate and support. "Here is a man who will listen to problems. Here is a man who thinks as we do. Here is a man who will decide my case in my favor. David is out of touch. We need a new man. Three cheers for Absalom!"

Continuing on the campaign trail in Jerusalem, Absalom was a portrait of friendliness. Whenever he met someone, this person would normally bow in obeisance to the king's son and heir apparent (15:5). But Absalom would stop him, shake his hand, and give him a hug and a kiss (15:5). By doing this, he became "one of them." His open "friendliness" was in marked contrast to David's seclusion in the palace. (David was lying on a sickbed during much of this time. See Psalm 41:3.)

Using these clever schemes, Absalom *"stole the hearts of the men of Israel" (15:6)*. This word for *"stole"* conveys the meaning of taking what belongs to another without consent, secretly. Often it involved deception. Interestingly, this word is used in the prohibition found in the eighth commandment, *"Thou shalt not steal" (Exodus 20:15)*. Absalom had the people in the palm of his hand. He was now ready to carry out his plan.

Masterminding a Devious Plan (15:7-12)

How long did it take Absalom to plan and implement his rebellion? Our text (KJV) reads, *"After forty years."* However, this appears to be a logical impossibility. If we consider this number as Absalom's age, we encounter a major problem. Absalom was born when David was in his early thirties (3:2-3; cf. 5:4-5). Adding forty years would make David over seventy. Since David died after a forty-year reign, he died at age seventy (I Kings 2:10-11). Nor could the number be from the time of Absalom's return to Jerusalem, for this would place David's age near one hundred! It could not be the fortieth year of David's reign because there would be a maximum of six months to cover the remaining events of II Samuel. That it could be David's age is out of the question since Absalom would be only about eight years old and still said to have a grown daughter (14:27)! Besides, the years have to relate to Absalom, not David, because of the context. At this point we are grateful that God has allowed His Word to be preserved in other manuscripts of other languages. The Syriac as well as the Septuagint state the period as being *"four years,"* not forty. This number fits very well into the circumstances. The rebellion climaxed either four years after Absalom's return to Jerusalem or four years after the "reconciliation" between Absalom and David.

After four years of plotting, Absalom approached his father and asked permission to travel to Hebron to fulfill a vow (15:7). Supposedly while in Geshur, Absalom promised God that if he were allowed to return to Jerusalem, he would make a pilgrimage to Hebron to sacrifice (15:8). From our perspective we readily recognize the deception in Absalom's words. His going to Hebron was only the first step in a five-step plan to overthrow David's government. But why did he want to go to Hebron? Let me suggest four reasons. First, Hebron was a day's journey from Jerusalem; this would give Absalom freedom to operate. Second, David had been anointed there. Absalom therefore concluded the next king should be anointed there. Third, the people of Hebron might still be smarting from David's action in moving the capital from Hebron to Jerusalem. Absalom could find the support he needed from these discontented citizens. Fourth, Absalom had been born in Hebron, and the local people might favor a native son's being king.

Several years ago Arnold Palmer from Latrobe, Pennsylvania, went to Florida and bought a piece of property in the town where a professional golf tournament was to be held the next week. It just so happened that he won the tournament. On the following morning the headlines read, "Local Boy Makes Good." A similar feeling of "local boy makes good" would appeal to the men of Hebron.

Step two of Absalom's plan was the sending of advance men *("spies")* throughout Israel (15:10). This speaks of footmen who go to and fro examining and evaluating. Their duty was to find Absalom's crowd and secure their loyalty.

Step three was the establishing of a line of communication for the takeover (15:10b). At strategic locations through the land, men were stationed with rams' horns. When everything was ready, a signal would be sounded in Hebron which would be relayed throughout Israel. Simultaneous with the sounding was to be a proclamation and celebration of the ascension of the new king.

The fourth step in Absalom's plan was the dividing of David's known support (15:11). This was accomplished by inviting two hundred of the king's court officers to go to Hebron with Absalom. These men were totally ignorant of Absalom's plot to oust David.

The fifth and final step involved the procuring of a man who could provide a smooth transition from one king to the next. Absalom found a likely candidate in Ahithophel, who was well known for his wise counsel (II Samuel 16:23). Perhaps he had helped Absalom map out the entire strategy for the treason. When we discover him, he is in his home town of Giloh, located south of Hebron, where he is offering sacrifices (15:12). Why would Ahithophel betray his life-long companion, David? Some have suggested that Ahithophel was Bathsheba's grandfather and that his son Eliam was a fighting comrade of Uriah (11:3; 23:34). If this be the case, then Ahithophel may have been motivated by bitterness. Certainly Ahithophel was looking for a place of greater prominence in the kingdom. His desertion was a source of great heartache for David (Psalm 41).

"And the conspiracy was strong; for the people increased continually with Absalom" (15:12b). "Conspiracy" means to bind something to something. These wicked men had made a pact, a league with one another, to destroy David. The stage was set; the characters were in place. All listened eagerly for the sound of the rams' horns which would raise the curtain on tenth century B.C. tragedy.

Reflecting on the character and actions of Absalom, we are drawn to the conclusion: Watch out for troublemakers! We will all encounter them from time to time. Our duty is to spot and avoid them at all costs. Absalom displayed five characteristics which are evident in all troublemakers.

1. They are *sensational* (v. 1)! Troublemakers are known for their ability to put on a show. They can make the Rose Parade wilt with envy. They are enamored with their own greatness and gifts.

2. They are *critical* (v. 3)! Troublemakers have difficulty seeing the good in anything. They are often found in the corner with a disgruntled soul, questioning the authority of others. To them the leader can do nothing right.

3. They are *egotistical* (v. 4)! Troublemakers have all the answers. They gloat over the inability of others, while whining, "I wish I had a chance." These people believe they are God's gift to mankind.

4. They are *Pharisaical* (vv. 7-8)! Troublemakers place a heavy emphasis on what they do rather than what they are. They can talk spirituality with the best of

theologians, but a close examination of their lives reveals empty words.

5. They are *artificial* (vv. 5-6)! Just as Absalom's friend-liness was a put-on, so are the actions of trouble-makers. They lush and gush over people, but they are as phony as a three-dollar bill.

Have you seen any troublemakers lately? If you have, you had better steer clear. They have an uncanny abil-ity to wreck the lives of anyone who ventures near.

TIMELESS TRUTHS FOR TODAY

---

1. You can become a troublemaker before you know it—keep on the alert.

2. You can spot a troublemaker a mile away—keep the distance between you.

Chapter 18

Encouragement in a Dark Hour
II Samuel 15:13-37

Let's play a game.

What do the following men have in common: Cain, Hophni, Phinehas, Joel, Abiah? Give up? Try two words. Rebellious sons! Cain was the first child ever born but rebelled when he got caught up in "doing his own thing." Hophni and Phinehas rebelled when a father failed to use loving restraint and discipline. Joel and Abiah were another pair of brothers who rebelled. Their problem was a fleshly focus on material values and a thirst for *things*. Behind each of these sons, hovering in the shadows, is a brokenhearted dad with tearstained face. Meaningful relationships had eroded through years of neglect, leaving telltale lines of wear and worry etched on the human clay. Sounds much like current family conditions in America, doesn't it?

"Emotion packed" is the only way to describe the situation of Absalom's rebellion against his father.

141

Perhaps some had seen the "handwriting on the wall" well in advance, but somehow David could not bring himself to believe that his oldest living son would turn traitor and turn from everything for which his father stood. Yet the facts are all there in full view of anyone who cares to examine them. Absalom had carefully designed and executed a plan to take possession of the throne of Israel. An aging dad was left little choice— remain and resist or run and regroup.

David: Running from Absalom (15:13-18)

Panic must have gripped the hearts of David's servants when they realized what had taken place. It was apparent that the multitudes had been swayed by Absalom's treachery. When news reached David (15:13), his words were quick and decisive. The king's servants were to flee from the city with the king (15:14). The reasons for this move were obvious. First, this course of action would avert civil war and spare the people from needless bloodshed. Second, escaping from Jerusalem would protect the city from the inevitable destruction that accompanies conflict. These two ideas are stated in as many words in verse fourteen. A third reason could have been that David wanted to buy some time. Leaving the capital was the only way this could have been assured. Fourth, David possibly reasoned that he would have a better chance at winning in open territory where he and his men were well experienced instead of being forced to fight in the restraining confines of a city. And finally, by withdrawing from Jerusalem, he could easily identify his loyal supporters as those who would leave their homes to follow him.

Although the hour was dark (figuratively speaking), a few spots helped light the way. One of these is recorded in verse fifteen. David's servants responded, *"Behold, thy servants are ready to do whatsoever my lord the king shall appoint" (15:15).* That must have encouraged David. He knew he did not have to face this crisis alone.

The Hebrew word for *"appoint"* means to take a perceptive look at something, to examine carefully in order to make a good choice. That is a necessary quality in leadership—to be able to make decisions based on what will be most beneficial and least harmful for all involved. David's men were responsive to that sort of thoughtful leader.

Quickly the royal and loyal families gathered a few necessary items and headed toward the Kidron Valley. Absalom would soon arrive and would surely destroy anyone who faltered in support of the new regime. When David vacated the palace, he left ten concubines to look after the upkeep (15:16). This clearly shows that David intended to return. His remaining family went with him to the edge of town. The phrase, *"a place that was far off" (15:17),* is literally translated "at the most distant house." This was a logical, well-known meeting place for those who had committed themselves to follow David. Included in the assembly were the Cherethites and the Pelethites—the royal bodyguard (cf. 8:18)—and six hundred men who are called Gittites (men of Gath). These six hundred are not to be considered as Philistines so far as their national origin is concerned. The writer has identified them as the men who *"came after him* [David] *from Gath" (15:18).* Four hundred joined David in a cave when he fled from Saul (I Samuel 22:1-2). An additional two hundred united with the corps by the time David left Keilah (I Samuel 23:13). This army came with him to Hebron in 1011 B.C. when David was crowned king in Hebron (II Samuel 2:3) and helped to conquer and establish

Jerusalem as the new capital (II Samuel 5:6). They had been through thick and thin with their leader, but their loyalty was undiminished. When David was forced to "hit the road," his six hundred did not balk for a moment. They had been there before; they would gladly do it again.

David: Receiving Encouragement (15:19-23)

Even though David was a strong leader yielded to God's will, leaving his home—his throne—must have been a heartbreaking experience. It seems that at those times God sends along a special encouragement to give strength to face the problem. With David, the encouragement came in the form of a "Johnny-come-lately" with an unforgettable name—Ittai the Gittite.

As Ittai passed before the king, David stopped him and asked, *"Why do you, indeed you, go with us?"* (literal translation, 15:19). Of all people, why should Ittai commit himself to follow David? He was a stranger and an exile (15:19). He had only recently come to Jerusalem with his family (15:20). The king attempted to send him back with the blessings of kindness and faithfulness.

Ittai's reply was initiated with a double oath—one to Jehovah and the other to the king. *"Surely in what place my lord the king shall be, whether in death or life, even there also will thy servant be"* (15:21). The phrase *"whether in death or life,"* demonstrated Ittai's firm resolve to stand by David. Talk about encouragement! Those words from a stranger's lips were like a soothing ointment on the open wound of discouragement. (When was the last time you soothed the wounds of a discouraged friend?)

Fighting back the tears of gratitude, David sent Ittai on ahead with the rest of the crowd. Ittai was followed by *"all of his men, and all the little ones that were with him"* *(15:22)*. The writer has painted a moving word-picture for us in the reference to *"little ones."* The Hebrew word means "to trip, to take quick little steps." Although the term could refer to anyone between the ages of birth to twenty, normally it speaks of tots. As David watched Ittai's procession, he saw the families of Ittai and his men, little children just learning to walk, stumbling, tripping, pattering their tiny feet along the dusty path to the wilderness. The reality of the devotion of these families must have gripped David's heart. It was a touching moment. Those who looked on wept loudly at the sight of the king, his followers, and their families, crossing the Kidron Valley, heading for an unknown destination (15:23).

David: Relying on God (15:24-31)

Zadok and Abiathar, who were serving as high priests in the sanctuary of God, had brought the ark from the city to the Kidron Valley. Having set down the ark, Abiathar offered sacrifices (KJV *"went up"*) while the people crossed the brook. David saw what was happening and called for Zadok, whom he instructed to take the ark back to its appointed place. The ark symbolized the presence of God and had often been transported with the people of Israel into difficult situations where God's assistance was desired. But David did not consider the ark as a relic or "good luck charm" whereby he could force God's blessing and presence to accompany him. Instead, the sweet psalmist of Israel displayed an attitude of sweet surrender as he laid bare his heart and said, *"If I shall find favor in the eyes of the Lord, he will bring me again, and shew me both it, and his habitation: But if he thus say, I have no delight in thee; behold, here am I, let him do to me as*

seemeth good unto him" (15:25-26). To get a better picture
of what is stated, let me explain two words. *"Favor"* (v.
25) is actually the word *grace*. For David to be allowed to
return to the city and worship God before the ark
would have to be a matter of grace. The second word is
"delight," meaning an emotional delight in someone,
based upon his intrinsic qualities. David was inviting
God to examine his heart and life to see if he were still
"a man after God's own heart" (cf. Psalm 139:23-24; I Samuel
16:7). If God found David lacking in those essential
godly qualities necessary to please God, David resigned
himself to God's righteous judgment. He was willing
for God to mold, shape, or even mar his life. There is
only one word to describe David's spiritual character at
this critical stage in his life—impressive!

Obeying David's orders, Zadok and Abiathar returned to Jerusalem with their two sons, Ahimaaz and
Jonathan, respectively. There they would serve God
and assist David as informants. David was heading for
the fords of the Jordan River, located a short distance
to the north of Jericho. When Zadok learned any valuable information concerning Absalom, he was to pass
that along to David (15:28).

After Zadok and Abiathar left, a weeping David
climbed the Mount of Olives with covered head and
bare feet, a symbol of humility and mourning before
God (cf. Esther 6:12; Ezekiel 24:17). Near the top David
learned that Ahithophel had betrayed him and joined
with Absalom (15:31). David's hurt over Ahithophel
was later recorded in a psalm (41:9). Rather than
retaliate, he turned his problem over to God, praying,
*"O Lord, I pray thee, turn the counsel of Ahithophel into
foolishness"* (15:31). Little did David realize how quickly
God would answer that prayer.

David: Reasoning with a Friend (15:32-37)

After praying, David continued his climb to the top of Mount Olivet, where he was met by an old friend, Hushai the Archite (15:32). For years this man from a small town on the border between Ephraim and Benjamin had been a companion and advisor to the king. Unlike Ahithophel, Hushai was loyal and presented himself with torn garment and earth on his head. The use of earth on the head was symbolic of the recognition that we are all made of dust and should never forget the pit from which we were digged (cf. Psalm 40:2). Here was the answer to David's most recent prayer.

David reasoned that Hushai would be a burden if he decided to travel with David (15:33). This might have been due to his advanced age. As an alternative, David asked Hushai to return to the city and pretend to be Absalom's servant. Hushai would be able to frustrate and invalidate (KJV *"defeat"*) the counsel of Ahithophel by offering opposite counsel (15:34). Hushai would also be able to supply David with inside information concerning the situation at Jerusalem (15:35). This information could be relayed to Zadok and Abiathar, who would send their sons as messengers to David (15:35-36). Although not a part of Hushai's original intentions, he willingly altered his plans in order to serve David. He journeyed back down the mountain, across the valley, and entered the city just as Absalom arrived (15:37).

One word occurs six times in this section of Scripture, revealing to us the major theme. The word is *"servant."* What a contrast to the troublemaker found in the first twelve verses of chapter fifteen! Examining the lives of these servants, I find four qualities that are displayed by true servants under any circumstances.

Servants are dependable, pliable, humble, and available. Let's look briefly at this virtuous quartet.

When all seemed hopeless, David's servants came through (15:15, 18, 21), whether it was members of his court, his six hundred comrades-at-arms, or a new-comer like Ittai the Gittite. These had cast their lot with David even if it meant death (15:21). David had servants who were dependable.

Webster defines *"pliable"* as "flexible, yielding, adapt-able." That is exactly David's attitude as God's servant in verses twenty-five and twenty-six. He was not forc-ing God to fit his plans and wishes; he was totally yielded to be God's handiwork. I am reminded of Jeremiah's visit to the potter's house, where he observed that *"the vessel that he* [the potter] *made of clay was marred in the hand of the potter; so he made it again another vessel, as seemed good to the pot-ter to make it (Jeremiah 18:4).* Then God said, *"Behold, as the clay is in the potter's hand, so are ye in mine hand" (Jeremiah 18:6).* Unfortunately, most Christians are hardened and rigid and refuse any reshaping by the Potter.

Humble—certainly a forgotten quality. David learned it the hard way, as many of us do (15:30). But until we humble ourselves, there can be no exaltation (James 4:10; I Peter 5:6).

Servants can be used only if they are available. What impresses me most about Hushai is that he did not demand to serve David a certain way. Surely, he had his ideas, but when David desired a different path, Hushai did not flinch or give "umpteen" excuses. He was available to be used as a servant.

And how about you? Are you wanting to be useful in God's service? Are you tired of living in the doldrums of status quo? If so, try harmonizing the quartet of dependability, pliability, humility, and availability into a song of service for the glory of God.

TIMELESS TRUTHS FOR TODAY

1. True servants are dependable.

2. True servants are pliable.

3. True servants are humble.

4. True servants are available.

Chapter 19

How to Handle Criticism
II Samuel 16:1-14

Unless you are inhuman or from another world, you have probably experienced in this past week a malady which is common to all mankind—discouragement. Maybe you have faced one or more of the following discouraging circumstances.

☐ You went in to ask the boss for a raise and left with a "pink slip."

☐ You weeded the garden but later discovered you had pulled up the plants instead!

☐ You became deeply involved in a thrilling "who-done-it" mystery and arrived at the crucial final chapter, only to discover it missing.

☐ You contracted athlete's foot, and you are not even an athlete!

☐ You hid an important document in an unforgettable place that you forgot.

☐ You brought home an anniversary gift for your

wife, only to find out that your anniversary was last week!

☐ You went to the supermarket. (Enough said!)

Regardless of the discouragement you have encountered, the most important question is, "How did you handle it?" In the crucible of affliction God grinds away the powder of pride and leaves us with indestructible character of true godliness.

David faced a difficult trial when his son Absalom betrayed his father and cunningly seized the kingdom for himself. David had every reason to be discouraged, but God surrounded him with loyal friends such as Ittai the Gittite, the court officials, and Hushai the Archite. Although he weathered that storm on this side of the Mount of Olives, a greater tempest awaited on the far side of the mountain. It often does. After a brief encounter with a shrewd servant, David was severely tested by an unbridled, unforgiving Benjamite by the name of Shimei. If ever anyone had reason to become discouraged, it was David. How would he handle it?

Ziba's Manipulation of David (16:1-4)

The chapter opens with David and his friends continuing their flight from Jerusalem down the east side of the Mount of Olives (16:1). Waiting for David to arrive was Ziba—a former servant of Saul and the present servant of lame Mephibosheth. Two donkeys, a hundred bunches of raisins, another hundred summer fruits, and a skin of wine had been brought by this cunning servant as a present for the fugitive king. When questioned by David as to the meaning of those provisions, Ziba informed the king that this was a gift to the king to make the journey easier. In fact, Ziba had provided a little something for everyone. The donkeys were for the king's family to ride on; the fruits were for the soldiers and servants; and the wine was for those who became weary in the heat of the desert (16:2).

Puzzled by the absence of Mephibosheth, David asked concerning this one to whom he had shown *"the kindness of God" (II Samuel 9)*. Ziba's answer must have struck the king in the heart. *"Behold, he abideth at Jerusalem: for he said Today shall the house of Israel restore me the kingdom of my father" (16:3)*. How could Mephibosheth say such a thing? Or did he? I believe Ziba was manipulating David in order to secure the favor of the king. In reality, Mephibosheth was innocent. Let us consider several pieces of evidence. First, Ziba had not been excited about serving a lame grandson of Saul (9:3). There was no prestige involved; neither was there hope of climbing the ladder of success. Second, when Mephibosheth came to Jerusalem, Ziba lost control over Saul's inheritance and his own independence (9:9-10). Third, since Ziba and his master lived near the king (he ate continually at the king's table), why did Ziba meet David on the far side of Olivet instead of in Jerusalem? Possibly Ziba was hiding his craftiness from those who could reveal his true intentions. Also, no one could testify against him to Absalom. Fourth, if Ziba were loyal to David, why did he not follow David into the wilderness rather than return to his reward in Jerusalem (16:4; cf. 19:15-17)? And finally, Mephibosheth later verified Ziba's deception against him (19:26-27).

Regrettably the king failed to see through the sham, and he compensated Ziba's "faithfulness" by transferring Mephibosheth's possessions over to Ziba. Several factors entered into David's using bad judgment. He was under emotional pressure because of Absalom's treachery. Undoubtedly David was suffering from a persecution complex, thinking everyone was against him. Emotional stress also built as David worried over the welfare of his family and friends. Add to this the physical strain. The emotional tensions were taking their toll physically, and David had just climbed a mountain. Remember that David was approximately sixty years old. He was not accustomed to running up and down those hills. Adding to the problem was the time factor. David had to make a quick decision without having time to check out the facts. Consider, too, that the gift Ziba was offering was very much needed at the time. Our wants often cloud good judgment.

Upon hearing the king's decision, Ziba bowed courteously, and with a smile on his face, returned to Jerusalem to claim his prize (16:4). His plan had worked. Mephibosheth was "out"; Ziba was "in."

Shimei's Humiliation of David (16:5-14)

On the road to Jericho and the Jordan, this caravan of refugees passed the little town of Bahurim (16:5), a Benjamite city. Some of Saul's relatives lived there, including Shimei. When Shimei saw David fleeing, he took advantage of the situation and vented his anger and frustration against the king. Shimei's attack came in four forms: name calling, false accusation, public shame, and physical assault.

Shimei picked up stones, threw them at David, screamed, "Get out, get out," and called him a *"bloody man"* and a *"man of Belial."* The title *"bloody man"* implicated David with the death of Abner (3:27-39), Ishbosheth (4:1-12), and Uriah (11:15-27). Shimei might be blaming the king for the death of Saul as well. The name of *"man of Belial"* is even more cruel. *"Belial"* is a compound of two Hebrew words, the first meaning "to become old, worn out"; and the second, meaning "profit, gain." Shimei was saying, "David, you are worthless, worn out, good for nothing." Whoever thought up the proverb, "Sticks and stones may break my bones, but words will never hurt me," never felt the sharp pain of verbal abuse.

Shimei's attack also contained false accusation. Besides being accused of the death of Saul's house, David was charged with usurping the throne (16:8). All the problems David now encountered were viewed by Shimei as God's divine judgment on a bloody man. Shimei must have considered himself an instrument of God's vengeance, for he took it upon himself to make a physical assault against David and his party. The text states that Shimei *"cast stones at David" (16:6)*. The word in the original is used of stoning someone to death. If he could have, Shimei would have killed David. But thank God that when the "stones" of criticism and false accusations were being cast, David found himself surrounded and protected by a band of loyal friends. Notice verse six: *"And he cast stones at David, . . . and all the people and all the mighty men were on his right hand and on his left."* Amazing! What a tribute! Rather than letting David be exposed and injured, these people lovingly encircled the one being harassed. What a beautiful picture of God's purpose for the church as a place of refuge from the attacks of the world!

All of this public shame, humiliation, accusation, and criticism could have left David defeated, despondent, and discouraged. How did he handle it? David exemplifies for us four reactions to criticism and false accusation.

1. Endure patiently . . . Don't get even! Abishai, the brother of Joab, was one of David's generals. He stood close by David during this incident. He was often involved in killing or the desire to kill (cf. I

Samuel 26:6-9; II Samuel 3:30; 19:21; 21:17). His answer to Shimei's abuse was to relieve the man of ten pounds of ugly fat by removing his head (16:9). David's reply was, *"What have I to do with you, ye sons of Zeruiah?"* In other words, "What do we have in common? Our philosophies are poles apart." David was the man after God's own heart. Abishai was the man after somebody's head. David was trying to teach his men that you do not get even with your enemies. Benjamin Franklin put it well when he said, "Doing an injury puts you below your enemy; revenging one makes you but even with him; forgiving it sets you above him."

2. Accept willingly . . . Don't get mad! David's surrender to God and acceptance of Shimei's criticism is admirable. *"So let him curse, because the Lord hath said unto him, Curse David . . . Let him alone, and let him curse; for the Lord hath bidden him"* (16:10, 11). The hardest thing in the world is to accept criticism. David saw the criticism as a tool of God to shape his life further for future good. This leads us to a third necessary reaction.

3. Judge honestly . . . Don't get defensive! Human nature craves to be justified of guilt. Six words we all hate are, "I am wrong," "I am sorry." Although David was innocent of the charges, he was motivated to look deeper into the situation and into his own life. Rather than condemning Shimei for what was taking place, he excused him. *"Behold, my son, which came forth of my bowels, seeketh my life: how much more now may this Benjamite do it?"* (16:11). That is good logic. If God permitted Absalom, David's son, to criticize his father, why should not someone else? Then David revealed the true reason for Absalom's rebellion and Shimei's reviling. David was reaping

the judgment for his sins against Bathsheba and Uriah. In verse twelve David talks about *"mine affliction."* Literally the word is *"iniquity."* God was fulfilling the sentence pronounced by Nathan that suffering and shame would haunt David and his family (12:9-10). David saw the righteous hand of God purging him of sin and guilt.

Suppose David had been guilty of the accusations made by Shimei. God's word offers this advice, *"Confess openly."* But David was blameless. Therefore, his fourth reaction was proper.

4. Commit totally . . . Don't get discouraged! David turned the whole matter over to God. *"It may be that the Lord will look on mine affliction* [iniquity], *and that the Lord will requite me good for his cursing this day"* (16:12). David believed that if he kept his attitude right and committed himself to God's mercy and grace, God would eventually bless him for it. He could have become discouraged and given up, but his trust in his Lord kept him going.

As David shared these life-changing principles with his men, Shimei continued his cursing and stone-throwing antics (16:13). Finally, they moved beyond Bahurim and proceeded to a caravansary near the Jordan where they refreshed themselves from the long, hot journey through the desert.

"You have come a long way, David." Years ago he had been similarly criticized and abused by a fool named Nabal (I Samuel 25); his reaction then, *"Gird ye on every man his sword"* (I Samuel 25:13); his reaction now, *"Let him alone"* (16:11). Quite a difference! No, he was not yet perfect, but throughout his life he had grown in his relationship with God. His heart beat in sympathy with God's heart so that his reaction became like that of God's Son, of whom it is said, *"Who did no sin, neither was*

*guile found in his mouth: Who, when he was reviled, reviled not
again; when he suffered, he threatened not; but committed himself to
him that judgeth righteously"* (I Peter 2:22-23).

Have you heard some criticism lately? Has someone
been falsely accusing you? Take David's advice—
endure patiently, accept willingly, judge honestly, and
commit totally. You will not only follow David's
example but also follow in the steps of Christ.

TIMELESS TRUTHS FOR TODAY

How to Handle Criticism:

1. **Endure patiently . . . Don't get even!**

2. **Accept willingly . . . Don't get mad!**

3. **Judge honestly . . . Don't get defensive!**

4. **Commit totally . . . Don't get discouraged!**

20

Where Are You, Lord?

II Samuel 16:15—17:23

An anonymous author has left for us a parable that is both comforting and encouraging. He entitled it—"Footprints."

"One night a man had a dream. He dreamed he was walking along the beach with the Lord. Across the sky flashed scenes from his life. For each scene, he noticed two sets of footprints in the sand, one belonging to him and the other to the Lord.

When the last scene of his life flashed before him, he looked back at the footprints in the sand. He noticed that many times along the path of his life there was only one set of footprints. He also noticed that it happened at the very lowest and saddest times of his life.

This really bothered him, and he questioned the Lord about it, 'Lord, You said that once I decided to follow You, You would walk with me all the way. But I have noticed that during the most troublesome times in my life, there is only one set of footprints. I don't understand why, when I needed You most, You would leave me.'

The Lord replied, 'My precious, precious child, I love you and I would never leave you. During your times of trial and suffering, when you see only one set of footprints, it was then that I carried you.' "

David could have profited from that little story. He was going through some of the deepest waters of his life. His family was disintegrating, his kingdom had been disrupted, and he himself was on the run. In fact, he was forced to cross the torrential Jordan during its floodstage in order to escape the vengeance of Absalom and protect the loyal band of friends who had followed him. Adding to his misery, David was continually badgered by those who mockingly asked, *"Where is thy God?" (Psalm 42:3, 10)*. Reading of these stages in the life of David does make one wonder. But God is there working behind the scenes to bring about His purposes. Where is God? Let's find out.

A Diplomatic Conversation (16:15-19)

When David had been informed of the sedition of Ahithophel, he had prayed that God would *"turn the counsel of Ahithophel into foolishness" (15:31)*. God made immediate provision for answer to that prayer when Hushai, another of David's counselors, offered himself in service to David. The king sent him back to Jerusalem with instructions to defeat the counsel of Ahithophel (15:34).

Before this could be done, Hushai had to win the confidence of Absalom. This was done through carefully chosen words. Hushai saluted David's son with the words, *"God save the king, God save the king"* (16:16), and probably did homage with the customary bow. Knowing of Hushai's former loyalty to David, Absalom expressed suspicion over Hushai's words. *"Is this thy kindness to thy friend* [David]? *Why wentest thou not with thy friend?"* (16:17). Absalom could not understand why Hushai would leave David at this critical moment.

The explanation which Hushai gives is a classic example of how you can hide double meanings in your expressions. He declared, *"Nay; but whom the Lord, and this people, and all the men of Israel, choose, his will I be, and with him will I abide"* (16:18). Obviously, Hushai believed that David was the chosen king, but his statement is understood by Absalom to mean that Hushai would be loyal to whoever was in power. Hushai further strengthened his position by saying, *"Whom should I serve? Should I not serve in the presence of his son? As I have served in thy father's presence, so will I be in thy presence"* (16:19). From all appearances, Hushai is lending credibility to Absalom's claim to the throne by pointing out that Absalom is David's son, the rightful heir. These words of Hushai must have been convincing, for Absalom accepted the old counselor as a member of his advisory staff.

A Daring Recommendation (16:20-23)

In these early stages of takeover, every move was critical. Absalom was smart enough to know that he needed to listen to his advisors. Ahithophel was asked to recommend the first steps to be taken to secure control of the kingdom. To the western mind, Ahithophel's counsel is bizarre. Absalom was told to pitch a tent on the roof of the palace and publicly be seen having sexual relations with David's concubines who had been left behind to keep the palace (16:21; cf. 15:16). In eastern culture, one way in which a successor claimed the right to the throne was by appropriating the harem of the former king (cf. 3:6-8). By this act Absalom would accomplish two results. He would cause a permanent division between David and himself. The text says that Absalom would be abhorred (literally "stink") of his father. The second consequence would be that Absalom's followers would be strengthened, realizing there was no turning back. It seems that Ahithophel would benefit most from Absalom's immoral act. Since Ahithophel had probably planned and instigated the plot against David, any reconciliation between father and son would cost Ahithophel his life. Therefore, the advice served to guarantee complete severance between David and Absalom. So Absalom followed the suggestion of his counselor and committed sexual acts with David's concubines (16:22).

Ahithophel wielded great influence in his lifetime. The reason for this is revealed in the closing verse of chapter sixteen. *"And the counsel of Ahithophel . . . was as if a man had inquired at the oracle* [literally "word"] *of God."* Wisdom was the hallmark of Ahithophel's words. He was able to discern what needed to be done and what steps of action were necessary to accomplish his ends. His advice could be trusted.

A Divided Opinion (17:1-14)

After Absalom's open immorality, Ahithophel approached his master with another recommendation. Ahithophel wanted the freedom to select twelve thousand men who would pursue and kill David that very night (17:1). Such quick action was important in order

to catch David while he was *"weary and weak" (17:2).*
These two words are descriptive of the emotional and
physical state of David and his men. *"Weary"* signifies
the exhaustion that attends hard labor or physical
strain. *"Weak handed"* comes from the Hebrew word
which means "to sink down, to let drop, to be disheartened." The image is that of a man whose hands drop to
his side because of weariness. In boxing terms we would
say, "He let down his guard." After the emotional strain
of rebellion and physical demands of a long march up
and down numerous hills, David and his troops would
be in no condition to defend themselves.

Escorted by twelve thousand fresh and zealous rebels,
Ahithophel would swoop down on the unsuspecting
prey, terrorizing and scattering them (17:2). In the confusion David alone would be killed, leaving the rest to
return unharmed to Jerusalem (17:2-3).

The most shocking statement of all appears in the
next verse. *"And the saying pleased Absalom well, and all the
elders of Israel" (17:4).* The original word for *"pleased"* means
"to be level, straight, just, lawful." Absalom and the
elders of Israel had degenerated so far in their rebellion
that they saw the death of David as the right or lawful
thing to do. The death of Absalom's father would
produce a level, smooth path for the acceptance of the
new king. You may be screaming right now, "Where is
God?" Be patient!

For no apparent reason, Absalom decided to see what
Hushai had to say about the matter (17:5). Although
hinting agreement with Ahithophel's previous counsel
(cf. 16:21), Hushai in essence said, "This time he is
wrong" (17:7). Using his words skillfully, he offered
four considerations for delaying the attack. First, he
reminded Absalom that his father and those with him
were mighty men (17:8). They knew how to fight.

These men were seasoned veterans in matters of war, while Absalom's men were relatively inexperienced. Second, Hushai pointed out that David's faithful were *"chafed in their minds"* or literally "bitter of soul" (17:8). Those guys are mad! This is illustrated by the picture of a bear robbed of her cubs. Their spirits would be ferocious. Only a fool would confront such an enemy. The third consideration Hushai gave was the fallacy in thinking David would be in camp with the people (17:8, 9). David knew the ways of war. He would not expose himself to sudden ambush. He would be hiding in a pit or some other concealed place, awaiting his opportunity to inflict the first blow. This brings us to the final concern of Hushai. Suppose David were to win the initial battle. The repercussions of defeat to Absalom's cause would be devastating (17:9). The most valiant of Absalom's warriors, even those who had the courage of a lion, would shrink back in fear of David (17:10).

What is Hushai's alternative? It is threefold. First, rather than twelve thousand men, assemble a vast army from every tribe from Dan to Beersheba (17:11a). Next, rather than letting Ahithophel get the glory, Absalom was to lead the armies himself (17:11b). Third, rather than killing just David, Absalom should wipe out the whole ungrateful lot (17:12). He should swallow them up, leaving no survivors. Using hyperbole, Hushai boasted that if David should hide in a walled city, that would be no problem. Absalom could tie ropes around the city and drag it to destruction in the valley until nothing was left (17:13). In those three suggestions, Hushai was appealing to Absalom's pride and his thirst for power. If Absalom swallowed this counsel, David would have time to retreat to further safety, organize his men, and recruit more help. Yet why should Absalom listen to Hushai when he already had the advice of Ahithophel? Read on.

"And Absalom and all the men of Israel said, The counsel of Hushai the Archite is better than the counsel of Ahithophel" (17:14). There must be some mistake! Any rational human being could plainly see that Ahithophel gave sound advice. Even the Bible admits this in the next phrase. But that next phrase also answers the questions, "Where is God?" and "Why did Absalom heed Hushai's counsel?" Notice it carefully, *"For the Lord had appointed to defeat the good counsel of Ahithophel, to the intent that the Lord might bring evil upon Absalom"* (17:14). On the surface it might not have appeared so, but God was there all the time. He is always in control.

A Dangerous Mission (17:15-22)

Employing the intelligence system previously established (cf. 15:28; 35-36), Hushai informed Zadok and Abiathar of the advice by Ahithophel and himself (17:15). Although Hushai's counsel was accepted by Absalom, Hushai still recommended that David immediately cross the Jordan for fear that Absalom might change his mind and pursue the former king (17:16). Jonathan and Ahimaaz, the priests' sons who were to be messengers to David, were given this news through a female servant. Jonathan and Ahimaaz had hidden themselves in one of the many caves surrounding the spring of En-rogel, located southeast of Jerusalem, where the Kidron Valley and Valley of Hinnom merge (17:17). This was a logical meeting place since it was some distance from the palace. En-rogel means "fountain of the feet" and was used by fullers as a place to tread their cloth. Women used the site to wash their clothes. The maid-servant could easily disguise her intentions for going there.

The plan seemed to be operating smoothly until a young lad spotted Jonathan and Ahimaaz and unraveled the mystery of what was happening. Quickly he reported to Absalom, who sent out a band of men to capture the spies (17:18). The priests' sons made it as far as Bahurim and realized they could not outrun the enemy. Finding a family whose sympathies lay with David, they sought hiding. In the courtyard of this man's home was a cistern used for storing water. Being large enough to serve as a refuge, Jonathan and Ahimaaz curled up within its walls. Wisely the lady of the house covered the top of the cistern (the opening was level with the ground) and spread grain over the top of the cover as if she were drying it (17:19). When Absalom's servants reached Bahurim, they happened to come to this very house (17:20). The moment was tense. The woman told the soldiers that the two men they sought had already crossed the brook and left the town. After an unfruitful search of the immediate area, Absalom's men returned to Jerusalem.

When the danger had passed, Jonathan and Ahimaaz came out of hiding and made their way through the wilderness to David's camp (17:21). By that time the shadows of darkness had moved across the landscape. David was told he must not delay in putting the Jordan between himself and Absalom. Recognizing the urgency of the situation, David moved his people through the raging torrents of the swollen Jordan during that dark night. By morning everyone had crossed safely (17:22).

Would you be interested in knowing David's thoughts as he looked over the scene the next morning? God has graciously preserved them for us in the forty-second and forty-third psalms. Surveying the foaming currents and listening to the roaring of the waters, he rejoiced, *"The Lord will command his lovingkindness in the daytime, and in the night his song shall be with me, and my prayer unto the God of my life" (Psalm 42:8).* David was alone, but he was not forsaken. Surely, he struggled with discouragement (Psalm 42:5). He was constantly confronted by the question, *"Where is thy God?" (Psalm 42:3, 10).* But his hope was firmly committed to his God (42:5, 11; 43:5).

A Deadly Conclusion (17:23)

Meanwhile, back in Jerusalem, Ahithophel was busy reading the handwriting on the wall. He knew that following Hushai's counsel would give David the opportunity to gather strength and organize his men. The defeat of Absalom was inevitable. Unwilling to face the consequences of his actions, Ahithophel journeyed to his hometown of Giloh, where he set his house in order. In shame and despair he took his own life by hanging (17:23). He had betrayed an innocent king, and guilt forced him to hang himself. Ten centuries later a similar traitor would betray a greater King from the house of David. He, too, would die at his own hands with a rope around his neck.

From these verses and the parallel psalms, I see three principles for putting our circumstances in perspective. The first is this: God is in control of every circumstance—good or bad! Ahithophel and Absalom appeared to have the upper hand. Many people were asking David, *"Where is thy God?"* Like a ray of light shining out of the darkness, Scripture records, *"For the Lord had appointed to defeat the good counsel of Ahithophel" (II Samuel 17:14).* Despite the appearance, God was at work. Do not kid yourself into thinking that God is not around when the going gets tough. He is just as concerned, just as real then as He is in the good times.

A second principle comes from Psalm 42: Every circumstance has two sides—dark and bright! Things looked dark for David, literally and figuratively. Listen to his cries—*"My tears have been my meat day and night . . . I pour out my soul in me . . . Why art thou cast down, O my soul? and why art thou disquieted in me? . . . Why hast thou forgotten me? . . . Why dost thou cast me off?" (Psalm 42:3, 4, 5, 9; 43:2).* Lots of sorrow. Lots of questions. Yet David saw a brighter side. He realized that his circumstances were learning experiences. He gained a greater appreciation for God. He learned to have a deeper trust in God. His recurring admonition to himself was, *"Hope thou in God"* (Psalm 42:5, 11; 43:5).

A third principle evident is this: Circumstances should not drive us *from* God but *to* Him. David's problems did not drive a wedge between him and his God. His problems served as glue to fasten himself to God. *"As the hart panteth after the water brooks, so panteth my soul after thee, O God. My soul thirsteth for God" (Psalm 42:1-2).*

What do you do when you are facing problems? David committed the matter totally to God and used his circumstances as a springboard for richer fellowship with God. That may not always be easy to do, but the benefits are eternal!

TIMELESS TRUTHS FOR TODAY

---

1. God is in control of every circumstance—good or bad!

2. Every circumstance has two sides—dark and bright!

3. Circumstances should not drive us *from* God but *to* Him!

Chapter 21

The Cry of a Broken Heart

II Samuel 17:24—18:33

Across the Jordan Valley to the east was an area known in Bible times as Gilead. Receiving heavy dews and ten inches of moisture a year more than the hill country on the west side of the Jordan, Gilead was a fertile, flourishing land. Rich farmlands, bountiful wheatfields and abundant grazing pastures made that region desirable for settling. This territory also boasted great oak forests and thick shrub bushes which were nestled among the hills, rising as high as four thousand feet, and deep in the ravines left from seasonal runoffs. Earlier in Israel's history this lush area had enticed the tribes of Reuben, Manasseh, and Gad to choose this location for their inheritance.

Dividing this expanse of land was the Jabbok River, providing an adequate water supply for local inhabitants. Near one of the fords and just to the north of this stream was a large, well-fortified town called Mahanaim.

Approximately two millennia before the Christian era, on his way to meet his brother Esau, Jacob had given the site the name Mahanaim, meaning "two camps" or "twin companies," when he encountered some angels of God. God was assuring Jacob of protection from his estranged brother (Genesis 32:1-2). Six hundred years later the city would be given to a group of Levites as a secure home for their families (Joshua 21:38). After Saul's death, Ishbosheth was established as Israel's king by Abner in the city (II Samuel 17:24). Mahanaim also became an important city in Solomon's administration (I Kings 4:14).

It was to this defensed city that David fled when threatened by his son Absalom (II Samuel 17:24). Absalom soon followed with his armies and a new military leader named Amasa (17:25). Once in the land of Gilead, Israel's troops set up camp and readied themselves to fight their former king—David (17:26). David, severely outnumbered and near exhaustion, threw himself upon the mercy of God. He cried, *"From the end of the earth will I cry unto thee, when my heart is overwhelmed: lead me to the rock that is higher than I. For thou hast been a shelter for me, and a strong tower from the enemy. I will abide in thy tabernacle for ever: I will trust in the covert of thy wings" (Psalm 61:2-4).* When David came to the end of himself, he found security in his God, and God delivered him from his enemies.

The Generosity of Three Friends (17:27-29)

The first and foremost problem facing David was the need of supplies. Josephus, the Jewish historian of the first century A.D., believed David's fighting men numbered four thousand. Although some men from the Transjordan joined his cause, many of these had come with their families from Jerusalem and its environs. But David had no way to provide bedding, housewares, or food for these loyal followers. At that critical moment God sent three friends to encourage David—Shobi, Machir, and Barzillai (17:27).

Shobi was the son of Nahash, the late king of Ammon. During David's fugitive years, Nahash had befriended the future king, a deed David never forgot (10:2). When Nahash died, his son Hanun, brother of Shobi, ascended to the throne (10:1). David attempted to comfort the grieving sons but was shamed when his ambassadors were treated with contempt (10:4). War ensued, and ultimately David won (12:29-31). Apparently, Shobi was appointed guardian of the Ammonite territory after the defeat. Perhaps he had willingly submitted to David's authority. Shobi's aid to David at Mahanaim displayed a deep-seated loyalty and revealed that he did not look upon David as Hanun his brother had.

Machir was a wealthy man who seemed to thrive on helping the underdog. In the ninth chapter of II Samuel we find him boarding Mephibosheth, the lame son of Saul (9:4). Machir's kindness to David grew out of David's kindness to Mephibosheth.

The third man mentioned was an eighty-year-old patriarch named Barzillai, whom we will meet again in a later chapter. He lived in a town in northern Gilead called Rogelim. His character is well depicted in the meaning of his name—"made of iron." No reason is suggested as to why he supported David. Undoubtedly, though, Barzillai was attracted to David's character. Maybe this is an ideal illustration of the proverb, *"Iron sharpeneth iron; so a man sharpeneth the countenance of his friend"* *(Proverbs 27:17)*.

These three provided David with *"beds, and basons, and*

*earthen vessels, and wheat, and barley, and flour, and parched
corn, and beans, and lentiles and parched pulse, and honey, and
butter, and sheep, and cheese of kine" (17:28-29).* Though
masters of large estates, these men were servants who
saw people with needs, were moved with compassion,
and were motivated to action (17:29).

The Strategy for the Upcoming Fight (18:1-5)

With one major worry out of the way, David turned
his attention to defending himself and his people. With
precision and speed, he mustered his forces and
organized them into three divisions—one under Joab,
one under Abishai, and one under Ittai the Gittite
(18:1-2). David's decision to lead his men into the field
was met with a strong protest from his generals (18:2-
3). They reasoned that David must not be vulnerable to
open attack and therefore should remain in Mahanaim.
Besides, David could lead a support group into the field
if need be. The king yielded to the advice of his men and
would anxiously await the outcome by the city gate
(18:4).

Before the warriors' final departure, David spoke to
his three commanders—*"Deal gently for my sake with the
young man, even with Absalom" (18:5).* These were hard
words for Joab and Abishai to swallow. Their style was
to kill first and ask questions later. Because David knew
that, it may have prompted his plea to treat his son
gently (or softly).

The Brutality of Joab and His Followers (18:6-18)

The two armies met in the treacherous woods of
Ephraim (18:6). Of the twenty thousand men slain of
Absalom's army, more were killed through accidents in

the woods than were slain by the sword (18:7-8).
David's men decisively routed their opposition.

Absalom had joined his men in the fighting but
evidently became separated from his soldiers. As he
passed through the woods on his mule, he met David's
troops face-to-face. In attempting to escape, he rode
under the thick boughs of a great oak. Suddenly his
head got caught in the limbs of the tree (18:9). Josephus
has popularized the theory that Absalom's long hair (cf.
14:26) entangled itself in the boughs; this is a
reasonable assumption. Absalom's frightened mule
continued his flight, leaving Absalom suspended
"between the heaven and the earth." The source of Absalom's
pride (his hair) had become the source of his downfall.

The young rebel must have been close to eluding the
men of David since the text implies only one man saw
Absalom's plight (18:10). The witness quickly informed
Joab of Absalom's bondage. In anger and disgust, Joab
rebuked the soldier for not having killed the enemy on
the spot. The soldier would have received a handsome
reward and trophy belt for such a deed (18:11).
However, this soldier exhibited integrity, for he
replied, *"Though I should receive a thousand shekels of silver in
mine hand, yet would I not put forth mine hand against the king's
son: for in our hearing the king charged thee and Abishai and Ittai,
saying, Beware that none touch the young man Absalom"* (18:12).
As a soldier, this man knew the importance of obedience. No amount of money would be sufficient to satisfy a guilty life and conscience. He knew that the king
would find out who had killed his son and would punish
the man. Even Joab would not have come to his defense
in such a case (18:13).

Joab had heard enough. Exasperated, he stated, "I'm
not going to waste my time here waiting on you" (cf.
18:14). He grabbed three spearlike shafts and proceeded

to the wood that held captive the king's son. Engaging in a game of "darts," with Absalom as the target, Joab must have recalled an earlier field fire and the bold demands of the brash young man (cf. 14:29-32). The scene took a further brutal turn as Joab allowed ten armor bearers to circle the writhing body of Absalom and mutilate him (18:15). For all practical purposes the rebellion was over. Joab sounded the retreat, marking an end to the bloodshed (18:16).

The remains of Absalom were taken to a deep pit close by, where he was deposited and then covered by a heap of stones (18:17). As the dust of the war settled, the writer gives a brief epitaph concerning Absalom's life. Absalom had erected a pillar in the king's dale (i.e., the Kidron Valley) in his own honor. He had no sons to carry on his name. (Obviously, his three sons mentioned in 14:27 died in infancy.) In order to be remembered, he built a monument known as Absalom's place (18:18). If you read between the lines of verse eighteen, you can find three words that summarize Absalom's life—loneliness, sadness, and emptiness. And he died as he had lived.

The Misery of a Bereaved Father (18:19-33)

All that remained to be done was to report to David the outcome of the battle. Ahimaaz, son of Zadok the priest, who previously along with Jonathan had delivered the urgent message that the king should hurriedly cross the Jordan, approached Joab and requested the honor of bearing the news (18:19). At first Joab refused to send the young runner because of the death of the king's son, and he indicated that Ahimaaz would have the opportunity on another day to serve David (18:20). Instead, Joab chose one of his own slave servants, a Cushite, to relate the events of the battle and tell of Absalom's death (18:21). After the Cushite's departure Ahimaaz again begged, *"But howsoever, let me, I pray thee, also run after Cushi" (18:22)*. A literal translation for the expression rendered *"howso-ever"* would be "and whatever it may be." This would be like saying, "Come what may, I want to run." Joab attempted to reason with the anxious youth, implying that there were risks involved in bearing the news of Absalom's death. Surely, there would be no reward (KJV *"ready"*) from the bereaved king (18:22). Nevertheless, Ahimaaz insisted and was allowed to run. Being a smart runner, Ahimaaz knew he could not catch the Cushite running through the thickets of the Ephraim woods. He decided to give up ground by taking a path that skirted the Jordan Valley. This plan presented few obstacles and proved to be a faster course as Ahimaaz overtook the Cushite near the city of Mahanaim (18:23).

David, who had been persuaded to remain in Mahanaim, waited in the court between the two gates (18:24). A watchman was surveying the area from the roof of the tower above the gate when he saw a runner (18:25). Since the runner was alone, David felt confident the news would be good (18:26). If David's forces had been defeated, many men would have been running to find shelter in the city.

Then a second runner appeared, and again David sensed that the news would be good (18:26). By this time the first messenger was nearing the gate, and the watchman was able to determine that the lead runner was Ahimaaz (18:27). Ahimaaz's first word to the king was, *"All is well,"* or *Shalom*. With that, he fell on his face and reported that Joab and the others were victorious (18:28). David, however, was not concerned about who won. He asked, *"Is the young man Absalom safe [shalom]?"*

Now Ahimaaz knew why Joab had hesitated to send him. Being careful not to offend the king or put himself in jeopardy, Ahimaaz lied, saying he had seen a big commotion but did not know what had taken place (18:29).

The Cushite had now arrived and was received by the king. This man also heralded David's conquest of his enemies, and again David inquired concerning the safety (literally *shalom*) of his son (18:31-32). Thinking the king would be pleased, the Cushite boasted, *"The enemies of my lord the king, and all that rise against thee to do thee hurt, be as that young man is"* (18:32).

The icy fingers of death left a chill on David's soul. His body began to shake, and his heart began to break. Seeking the privacy of the chamber above the gate, a broken father was heard crying, *"O my son Absalom, my son, my son Absalom! would God I had died for thee, O Absalom, my son, my son!"* (18:33). David had repeatedly asked about the safety (*shalom*) of his son but had learned instead of his death. David should not have been surprised. When the king had committed the situation to God, he prayed for justice, *"Judge me, O God"* (Psalm 43:1). God had answered that prayer, for twice in this passage it is recorded that David was avenged (18:19, 31). This is the same word that David used in his prayer in Psalm 43. He got what he prayed for but ended up with more than he bargained for.

David's mourning has been criticized by many through the centuries, but keep in mind that in that lonely chamber in Mahanaim stands more than a vindicated monarch. We find a bereaved father who realized he had failed his son and who had again felt the sting of the sword in his own house as a result of his own sin (cf. 12:10-11). What would you have done if you had been in David's shoes?

From this page in David's life let us make three practical observations. First, genuine friendship is triumphant in times of adversity. After David had crossed the Jordan and made his way to Mahanaim, he was destitute of necessary provisions. The situation was discouraging. In that hour of trial God graciously sent three friends to encourage and help (17:17-29). Job related his feelings when he stated, *"To him that is afflicted pity should be shewed from his friend" (Job 6:14a).* David's son Solomon worded it well when he wrote, *"A friend loveth at all times, and a brother is born for adversity" (Proverbs 17:17).* Are you a genuine friend?

The second observation I make is that genuine obedience is tested in times of opportunity. There is a striking contrast between Joab and an unnamed servant in verses ten through fourteen. The unnamed servant refused to excuse disobedience at any price. The opportunity to disobey lay before him, but his integrity restrained him. Face it, each of us is confronted daily with circumstances that tempt us to compromise the truth. How do you respond to the test?

The final observation from the passage comes from David's own life: Genuine love is tender in times of extremity. Who can doubt the agony David was going through? He was not simply a king without a throne; he was a father who had lost his home. His deep concern for his wayward son is evident throughout the story (18:5, 12, 29, 32, 33). David's life had been hard, but he was not hardened. His cries of anguish reveal the tender heart of a loving father who recognized his own failures in the life of his son. Have you found yourself at the point of extremity—at the end of your rope? Do not allow yourself to become bitter and hardened. Soak yourself in God's everlasting love. It will keep you tender in the tough times.

TIMELESS TRUTHS FOR TODAY

1. Genuine friendship is triumphant in times of adversity.

2. Genuine obedience is tested in times of opportunity.

3. Genuine love is tender in times of extremity.

Chapter 22

Learning Through Loss
II Samuel 19:1-39

Centuries ago there lived a man whose name has become synonymous with suffering. He lived in a land called Uz, a region southeast of the Dead Sea. Other references to this area identify the location with the ancient kingdom of Edom. The man's name was Job. He was noted for his integrity, his spirituality, and his innocency. Job had been blessed with a large family (ten children) and great herds of animals—a sign of his wealth. If you are unfamiliar with the story, you may be saying to yourself, "If that's a life synonymous with suffering, I'm ready for a little suffering myself." You had better consider scene two in the life of Job—he lost it all. The children died. The herds were destroyed. Even Job's good health was removed. How do you think he responded to loss? Bitterness? Cynicism? Anger? Listen to his own words: *"Naked came I out of my mother's womb, and naked shall I return thither: the Lord gave, and the Lord*

179

hath taken away; blessed be the name of the Lord" (*Job 1:21*).
Then the author of the Book of Job added this com-
ment, *"In all this Job sinned not, nor charged God foolishly"* (*Job
1:22*). Those are astonishing words.

Few people can handle loss with the maturity of a
Job. As a case in point, examine the life of David. The
Monarch of Israel had been driven from his palace in
Jerusalem and forced to seek refuge in the high country
of Gilead to the east of the Jordan. His enemy was his
eldest living son, Absalom. Conflict was inevitable, but
David warned his men to be careful not to hurt his
rebellious son (II Samuel 18:5, 12). However, in direct
opposition to the king's wishes, Joab and his armor
bearers killed and mutilated the prince. When David
learned of his son's death, grief overwhelmed him
(18:33). The tears of sorrow like an endless river flow
over into chapter nineteen. The victorious king seemed
unable to control his heartache.

Although II Samuel 19 has long been envisioned as a
chapter of triumph, there is another theme clearly
prominent—learning through loss. Let's take a fresh
look at an old story.

Rebuking David (19:1-7)

Four words in the opening verses describe the depth
of David's distress on this day—*"weepeth," "mourneth,"
"grieved,"* and *"cried" (19:1, 2, 4)*. Each word is vividly
expressive. *"Mourneth"* in verse one is generally used of
mourning rites for the dead. It is the ritual of remembering the dead usually accompanied by audible and
visible emotions. The audible emotions are depicted in
the word *"weepeth"* in the same verse, which was used of
loud shrieks or cries. David's agony is labeled as *"grief"*
in the second verse. This word presents the physical

pain that is often associated with sorrow. The final image of suffering is portrayed in the word *"cried."* The Hebrew root means to cry for help in time of distress. But the cry may be to no one in particular. It simply recognizes a need and pleads for help. With these four "strokes," the artist of this passage paints a picture of a grieving dad. The tones are dark, the shadows are long, and the canvas is blurred.

David's reaction to the death of his son was not hidden from his troops. From the open windows of the chamber above the gate were heard the cries of the despairing father (18:33). Rather than a victory celebration, a cloud of mourning hung low over the city (19:2). David's men actually tried to sneak unnoticed into the city because they were humiliated by the king's continued sorrow (19:3). Their actions are compared to those who *"being ashamed steal away when they flee in battle."* *"Ashamed"* is related to an Arabic word meaning "to wound" and depicts men of wounded pride.

Joab saw what David was doing to the morale of the soldiers and decided to confront the king (19:1, 5). Obviously he had not bothered to study any Dale Carnegie course on *How to Win Friends and Influence People.* In his typical unabashed style, he lashed out at the king, *"Thou hast shamed this day the faces of all thy servants . . . In that thou lovest thine enemies, and hatest thy friends"* (19:5-6). Joab pointed out that the lives of the rest of David's family had been spared because Absalom had been slain. If Absalom had lived and won the civil war, all descendants would have been executed according to eastern culture, thus insuring no rivals to the throne. Further, by David's actions, Joab presumed that *"if Absalom had lived, and all we* [David's men] *had died this day, then it had pleased thee well"* (19:6). Joab concluded his rebuke with a recommendation that David speak comfortably (literally "to the heart") of his servants; otherwise, wholesale dissertion would have taken place (19:7).

Uniting the Kingdom (19:8-15)

After being severely reprimanded, David followed Joab's advice and sat at the gate to encourage, thank, and congratulate his men on their valiant efforts against seemingly insurmountable odds. This was David's first step in regaining the confidence of his people and building a base to reunite the nation. Excitement and loyalty was restored as evidenced in the announcement, *"Behold, the king doth sit in the gate" (19:8).*

With his followers back in the fold, the exiled king turned his attention to winning the hearts of the men of Israel who had opposed him. Having been defeated on the battlefield, the Israelites who had backed Absalom fled to their tents (19:8). During Absalom's rebellion they had forgotten how faithful and successful David had been. He had been responsible for delivering them from their enemies on numerous occasions. Yet Absalom had convinced the general public to support him instead of David. Now that Absalom was dead, the men of Israel realized how foolish they had been and issued a call for David to return as king (19:10).

The tribe of Judah, however, was hesitant. Perhaps they feared David would avenge himself of their treachery. You will remember that the insurrection began in Judah's most notable town, Hebron (15:7 ff). Therefore, David took the initiative to rebuild the relationship between himself and Judah. Zadok and Abiathar, the priests, acted as the king's representatives to speak with Judah's elders (19:11). Specifically, David wanted to know why Judah was slow in submitting to the king, especially since the northern tribes had already asked David to come back. David also reminded them, *"Ye are my brethren, ye are my bones and my flesh" (19:12).* This would dispel any doubts concerning retaliation.

David also had to deal with the sensitive issue of what to do with Amasa, who had been commander of Absalom's forces (17:25). Because Amasa was from the tribe of Judah, the men of Judah would be watching closely to see how David handled the matter. In a turn of events that must have surprised everyone, David promoted Amasa to the position of head of his armies while stripping Joab of his power (19:13). Why David demoted Joab is explainable, considering two events. First, Joab had killed Absalom, expressly disobeying David's commands to the contrary. Second, David was still smarting from the verbal barrage loosed upon him by Joab earlier in this chapter. As to why Amasa was promoted, we can only conjecture that it arose out of political expediency in an attempt to mend further the division in the kingdom. His decision was unwise and nearly proved to be disastrous, as we shall see in a succeeding chapter.

Through these maneuvers, David was able to bow (i.e., turn, incline) the heart of the men of Judah and find unified support for his return (19:14). When the formal invitation was received, David and his servants packed up their families and headed for the Jordan, where a large welcoming party awaited (19:15).

Forgiving Shimei (19:16-23)

Among those who had journeyed to the Jordan Valley to meet David was Shimei of Bahurim (19:16).

Shimei was the man who verbally and physically assaulted David as the king left Jerusalem (16:5-13). But now he sang a different tune. Not wanting to wait for David to cross the Jordan, Shimei rushed through the swelling waters and fell down before the monarch (19:17-18). He pleaded for mercy and begged David to forget the foolish things he had done (19:19). Shimei frankly admitted, *"I have sinned" (19:20).* This is the most common word for *"sin"* in the Old Testament and means "to miss the mark." (A good illustration of this meaning is found in Judges 20:16.) It would be interesting to know if David might have pointed out a bruise from Shimei's rock-throwing days when Shimei had not "missed the mark."

Since Shimei had hurried to be the first to greet the king, he presented this fact as evidence of his humble and repentant heart (19:20). Abishai was unimpressed and believed Shimei was trying to wiggle out of a tight situation. Turning to the king, Abishai offered to kill Shimei because of his low esteem (KJV *"cursed"*) for David (19:21). David rebuked Abishai, saying that the sons of Zeruiah (Joab and Abishai) did not think as the king did, that such actions would bring further trouble, and that killing a subject on the day of the king's return would also kill the spirit of the people (19:22). Interestingly, David called the sons of Zeruiah adversaries (transliterated from the Hebrew language—"Satan").

David made an oath not to kill Shimei (19:23). Technically, David's refusal to kill Shimei was unjust, and implications from Scripture reveal that Shimei continued to be a thorn in David's side. Whatever else could be said of David's deed, we must give him credit for exhibiting a forgiving attitude to an undeserving man. God's people would do well to follow this example.

Confronting Mephibosheth (19:24-30)

Ziba, who had given some provisions to David when he left Jerusalem (16:1), was also at the Jordan to meet the king (19:17). However, Mephibosheth was present as well and hoped to clear his name of Ziba's slanderous remarks (16:3-4). Mephibosheth's appearance suggested his innocency. Since David's departure, he had not washed his feet, cared for his beard (literally "moustache"), or cleaned his clothes (19:24).

David asked the lame prince, *"Wherefore wentest not thou with me, Mephibosheth?" (19:25)*. Finally the true story came out. Mephibosheth had ordered his servant, Ziba, to saddle a donkey so that he could leave Jerusalem with the king. But Ziba seized the opportunity to promote his own cause, coming to David himself to send him off. When David and Ziba met near the crest of the Mount of Olives, Ziba lied to the king and was given all of Mephibosheth's possessions. Strangely, Mephibosheth demanded no restitution but, instead, only praised the king for his past mercies (19:28).

Realizing a mistake had been made, David restored to Mephibosheth half of the land, permitting Ziba to retain the other half (19:29). It is difficult to understand why David did not totally reverse his previous decision and give everything back to Mephibosheth. Some have proposed that David was still unconvinced of Mephibosheth's innocence. Maybe David's grief continued to cloud good judgment. Perhaps the king was not wanting to offend Ziba and cause further irritation in the fragile kingdom. The most remarkable episode in this encounter is that Mephibosheth declined to accuse David of any injustice. He even offered to let Ziba take all of the land. This gracious gesture supports his innocence. Mephibosheth was satisfied in knowing that David was once again king (19:30).

Leaving Barzillai (19:31-39)

Again we come face to face with a grand old man. From the heights of Gilead the eighty-year-old Barzillai came down to cross the Jordan with his friend, David. A special relationship must have developed between these two aged giants. Barzillai had been a chief supplier to David's army while they were in exile (17:27-29). While they walked in the valley, David asked Barzillai to leave his home and come to Jerusalem, where the king could care for his needs the rest of his life (19:33).

Barzillai had not only an abundance of wealth but also a full measure of common sense. He reasoned with David that his life was now far spent. At the age of eighty, the niceties of life did not mean much. His taste buds were not so lively. His hearing was diminished. The excitement of court life in the big city was not appealing. Barzillai looked forward to spending his twilight years in his own home and then be buried near the tomb of his parents (19:35, 37). He realized he would be a burden to David, and he did not want David to feel that he had to reimburse Barzillai for his kindness (19:36). Barzillai lived by the principle that expressions of genuine love need no repayment. David took Chimham, probably Barzillai's son, with him to Jerusalem and treated him kindly (19:37-38).

After Barzillai and David crossed the river, the two kissed and Barzillai blessed his king. Then they parted in opposite directions (19:39). Although they were separated physically by a great distance, these close friends were never separated in their spirits.

We stated at the beginning that this chapter teaches us the importance of learning through loss. May I suggest four things to be learned from this story? First, loss can temporarily cause us to lose our perspective (19:1-7). Although David was concerned about the death of his son, he forgot about the welfare of his friends and family. Loss and grief often cause us to lose sight of the total picture and focus only on self.

The second lesson to be learned is that loss can clearly cause us to remember God's provisions (19:9-10). The people of Israel did not realize what they had in David until they lost him and his inadequate replacement, Absalom. Isn't it amazing how a critical spirit robs us of a thankful spirit? During the rebellion nothing good was said about David. But when the thought of losing him gripped them, they remembered his greatness.

Third, loss can tenderly cause us to be sensitive to others' problems (19:22). Shimei could have been handled roughly within the realm of justice, but David's loss made him sensitive to Shimei's plea. Absalom's death kept David's heart tender to those who had need.

Finally, loss can ultimately cause us to appreciate God's people (19:33, 38). If David had not experienced loss, he would never have experienced the friendship of Barzillai. David's life was enriched through his association with the octogenarian of Rogelim. Reflect right now on your times of loss. Has God not given you some special friends during those dark hours? In the long run, times of loss do not make us poorer; they make us richer.

TIMELESS TRUTHS FOR TODAY

1. Loss can temporarily cause us to lose our perspective.

2. Loss can clearly cause us to remember God's provisions.

3. Loss can tenderly cause us to be sensitive to others' problems.

4. Loss can ultimately cause us to appreciate God's people.

23

Don't Lose Your Head
II Samuel 19:40—20:26

Someone has defined an argument as "something you do with a fool" but warned, "be sure he isn't similarly engaged." There are probably few activities in the world as foolish and futile as arguing. Benjamin Franklin observed, "Many a long dispute . . . may thus be abridged: It is so: It is not so: It is so: It is not so!" Very seldom does arguing accomplish anything except to widen the rift between two parties. One astute mind put it this way, "To win an argument is to lose a friend." Nowhere is this truth better illustrated than in the circumstances described in the closing verses of chapter nineteen of Second Samuel.

The Disunity Among the Tribes (19:40—20:3)

How quickly we tend to make a mountain out of a molehill! The relationship between Israel and Judah

melted away under the fires of a heated discussion over
an incidental matter. Clearly evident in the story are
six stages of deterioration. These stages roughly
parallel what happens in the course of most arguments.
Stage one—misunderstanding (19:40-41). The northern
tribes of Israel were the first to realize their error in
following Absalom's rebellion. In humility they invited
David to return as their king. Their southern brothers
had hesitated at first to issue a similar invitation, perhaps fearing some form of retribution from the king.
Yet they did finally submit to David's authority. For
some unknown reason, the southern tribe of Judah was
able to gather a welcoming party sooner than the northern tribes were. Therefore, when David crossed the
Jordan and passed by Gilgal, Judah was well represented
while Israel followed in a minority. On the road to Jerusalem the company of David met up with the rest of the
elders of Israel. The appearance of things was mis-
understood by the northern representatives which led
to . . . stage two—anger (19:42). The leaders of the ten
tribes of Israel were upset over what they saw. They
thought Judah was trying to take advantage of the situation and establish themselves in the king's favor. The
more they thought about it the more it angered (literally "burned") them.

Then came stage three—accusation (19:41). Rather
than getting the facts, the Israelites confronted the
king with an accusing question: *"Why have our brethren . . .
stolen thee away?"* Implied is a secret conspiracy between
David and Judah. Israel felt displaced. Jealousy developed. The temperature of the discussion began to rise.

Stage four—argumentation (19:42-43). Judah was
not satisfied to sit down and quietly settle the problem.
Their response drove a further wedge in the relationship. Although Judah explained they had taken nothing

from David nor had they sought any special favors, these men did refer to David as being their *"near of kin."* In essence Judah was arguing for her rights. The men of Israel were quick to point out that they had a greater right to David since their region was composed of ten tribes as opposed to two. Literally they said, "We have ten hands on the king." You can almost picture the raised fists and the shouts of anger.

Stage five—hurt feelings (19:43). The deeper emotions of the men of Israel is revealed in their question, *"Why then did ye despise us?"* The word *"despise"* means "to treat lightly, to hold in low esteem." The Israelites had been offended. David's son Solomon would later surmise, *"A brother offended is harder to be won than a strong city: and their contentions are like the bars of a castle" (Proverbs 18:19).* And the contentions grew *"fiercer"* (literally "hard, severe").

After the first five stages, the sixth was inevitable—division (20:1-2). Hanging around in the hostile crowd was a man waiting for his chance. Although his name, Sheba, means "oath," he was a man of disloyalty. He is described as *"a man of Belial,"* which was a polite way of calling him a scoundrel. When it became evident that the two sides were sharply divided, Sheba sounded the ram's horn and gained the attention of the multitude. With brash words he declared, *"We have no part in David."* Then he called for dissenters to retire to their tents to prepare for war (20:1; cf. I Kings 12:16). Rebellion had again reared its ugly head (20:2).

Surprisingly, David did nothing to restrain Sheba or reason with those who were divisive. David's passivity in facing problems was a characteristic of his later life. This helps us to understand why he encountered difficulties with his children. He was passive in his discipline.

From Gilgal the men of Judah *"clave"* (literally "stuck to, followed closely") to David until they reached Jerusalem (20:2). There David was reunited with his concubines. However, since they had been defiled by Absalom (16:21-22), the king shut them away in a private area as would be the case of widows (20:3). David might have done this to spare them of any further public embarrassment over what had been done to them.

The Delay in Gathering the Troops (20:4-13)

Amasa, the rebel general of Absalom who had been recently appointed as David's commander, was now given opportunity to show his loyalty to the king. David ordered him to assemble within three days an army that would overthrow Sheba's rebellion (20:4). But Amasa faltered in carrying out his duty within the specified time (20:5). Recognizing that further delay could prove disastrous, David directed Abishai, Joab's brother, to take a group of men and pursue Sheba (20:6). With Joab's personal guard, the Cherethites and the Pelethites, and David's mighty men, Abishai began his march northward (20:7).

Near the town of Gibeon, Amasa met the pursuers. When Joab saw Amasa, he cleverly devised a plan to kill his enemy. Arranging the sheath of his sword loosely upon his garment, Joab allowed the sword to fall to the ground as he went to give an official welcome to Amasa (20:8). The unsheathed sword was retrieved by the left hand while Joab used his right hand to grab Amasa's beard to kiss him. To kiss while holding the beard was a customary greeting. As Joab kissed his victim, he asked, *"Art thou in health, my brother?" (20:9).* He would not be for long! Amasa was not alert to Joab's intentions. With

one thrust Joab pierced the belly of Amasa and perhaps
drew the sword up and out (20:10). Amasa's internal
organs emptied out to the ground as Amasa himself fell
and agonized in pain. One of Joab's soldiers came to the
front and challenged the men to follow Joab and David
(20:11). But no one would cross over Amasa, who lay in
the middle of the road writhing in a pool of his own
blood (20:12). Therefore, the soldier dragged Amasa off
to the side and covered him with a cloth, and the men
followed Joab (20:13).

The Death of the Traitor (20:14-22)

Sheba had fled north from Gilgal and looked to find
support for his cause along the way (20:14). The only
people mentioned by name who followed him were the
Berites. This unknown group is found only here in all
of history. Together they traveled with Sheba to the
city of Abel of Beth-maachah, twenty-five miles north
of the Sea of Galilee and four miles west of Dan
(20:14). When Joab arrived on the scene, he and his
men went to work constructing a siege wall against the
city (20:15).

As David's men battered the wall, a commotion arose
within the city. The people were terrified. One wise
woman appeared at the top of the battlements and
asked to speak with Joab (20:16). Joab came and listened
to the woman. She appealed to Joab to spare the city for
several reasons. First, the people of Abel were noted
for their wisdom (20:18). Do you want to kill
productive citizens? Second, the citizens of this city
were peaceful and loyal to the king (20:19). Do you
intend to destroy innocent people? Third, Abel was one
of the major cities (KJV "mother in Israel") on the
northern frontier (20:19). Do you plan to remove an

outer defense? And finally, would Joab want to bear the responsibility of destroying *"the inheritance of the Lord" (20:19)?* Her wisdom was apparent, and Joab was defensive: *"Far be it, far be it from me, that I should swallow up or destroy" (20:20).* All Joab wanted was Sheba, the rebel. In her own sweet, tender way the woman stated, *"His head shall be thrown to thee over the wall" (20:21).*

Descending the wall, the wise woman told the people why Joab had besieged their city and advised them to search out Sheba and cut off his head. Soon the deed was done, and the head of Sheba came flying over the wall. But where were Sheba's "friends," the Berites? Obviously, their loyalty was not very deep.

Joab kept his promise and did not destroy the city. Having sounded the ram's horn, the soldiers returned to their homes, and Joab returned to Jerusalem with the traitor's head (20:22).

The Dignitaries About the Throne (20:23-26)

The chapter concludes with a list of officers surrounding David during his final years. As in the previous list found in the eighth chapter, Joab is still entrenched as the leader of Israel's armies (20:23). Benaiah continues to be over David's personal guard of the Cherethites and the Pelethites. Sheva (called *"Seraiah"* in 8:17) is still the scribe. The scribe is similar to our secretary of state. The priests remain the same—Zadok and Abiathar (20:25). Jehoshaphat is not mentioned (cf. 8:16).

Two changes have been made. Adoram has been installed as head of the tribute. Tribute here does not refer to money, but to forced labor gangs that carry on the building programs of the nation. This group would be used extensively in later days. The second change is that Ira took the places of David's sons as chief advisor to the king. This was necessitated by the fact that several of David's sons had been killed in the intervening years. Also, we might conjecture that David's previous experience with rebellion in his own family caused him to have second thoughts about placing his sons in high levels of the administration. How unfortunate!

If we were asked to describe in one word what this section of Scripture is all about, that word would be "rebellion." After meditating on these scenes, four truths about rebellion become prominent. First, rebellion rises out of disagreement (19:40-43). The arguments and anger were allowed to go too far. Second, rebellion reacts with disloyalty (20:1-2). Sheba never had been loyal to David. He was looking for an opportunity to thrust himself forward as an alternative to the king. Third, rebellion recruits the discontented (20:13-14). The Berites followed Sheba. They were unknown, unreasonable, uncaring young men who looked for trouble and found it. Fourth, rebellion results in disaster (20:22). Sheba paid for his sin with his life, and his name is forever recorded as "traitor." Rebellion may seem appealing at the outset, but its end is death and disgrace.

If you are facing a temptation to rebel or if you detect a rebellious spirit in others, may I offer a bit of advice. Handle rebellion as did the wise woman of Abel. Deal with it rationally, quickly, definitely, and with finality. Your life may depend upon it.

TIMELESS TRUTHS FOR TODAY

1. Rebellion rises out of disagreement.

2. Rebellion reacts with disloyalty.

3. Rebellion recruits the discontented.

4. Rebellion results in disaster.

24

Ordinary People
Who Became Giants
II Samuel 21:1-22

Uncovered in a tomb along the Nile was an inscription by an early Egyptian monarch relating the despair and suffering associated with famine.

"I am mourning on my high throne for the vast misfortune, because the Nile flood in my time has not come for seven years! Light is the grain; there is a lack of crops and of all kinds of food. Each man has become a thief to his neighbor. They desire to hasten and cannot walk. The child cries, the youth creeps along, and the old men, their souls are bowed down, their legs are bent together and drag along the ground, and their hands rest in their bosoms. The counsel of the great ones in the court is but emptiness. Torn open are the chests of provisions, but instead of contents there is air. Everything is exhausted."

197

The verbal picture painted by this king is hideous. However, one statement stands out in my mind: "The counsel of the great ones in the court is but emptiness." They were searching for answers, but none could be found. Drought, famine, and most other major disasters drive us to ask hard questions and probe deeper into the reasons why.

David found himself and his kingdom in the middle of a severe famine that had devastated the land for three consecutive years (21:1). Food supplies were running critically short. People were beginning to ask questions, but none of David's administration found quick answers or lasting solutions. Why it took David three years to inquire of the Lord about this matter, no one knows. But when he did, he found his answer (21:1).

The Vengeance of the Gibeonites (21:1-9)

The famine that plagued the land was a divine judgment upon the sin of Saul when he killed a group of Gibeonites (21:1). This tribe of people is introduced to us during the invasion of Canaan by Joshua in the fifteenth century before Christ. These Gibeonites, who lived within the borders of Canaan, feared destruction at the hand of Joshua; so they devised a plan to trick the Israelites into making a peace treaty with them. Having put on old clothes and having saddled their donkeys with stale provisions, they pretended to have journeyed from a far country (Joshua 9:3-20). Without seeking God's counsel, the princes of Israel made peace with the Gibeonites, only to discover three days later that they had been fooled. Although the Israelites had been commanded to destroy the inhabitants of Canaan, the Gibeonites were spared because of the covenant: *"We will even let them live, lest wrath be upon us, because of the oath which we sware unto them"* (Joshua 9:20; cf. II Samuel 21:2). Less than four hundred years after this event, Saul had massacred many of these people (21:5). Some believe this massacre was associated with the mass killing of the priests and townspeople of Nob (I Samuel 22:18, 19).

In order to restore God's blessing upon the land, atonement had to be made for the deaths of the Gibeonites (21:3). This is one of the most important passages in the Old Testament for understanding atonement. Our English word is actually a compound— *"at-one-ment"*—signifying the reconciling (bringing together) of two parties who have been at odds, and restoring peace between them. The Hebrew word is *kapar*. Once it was thought that the basic idea of this word meant "to cover." However, recent research has shown that to be incorrect. The primary definitions of this word include "payment of a ransom; make reconciliation." In almost all of the Biblical passages where *kapar* occurs, we find a substitution of money or life in order to appease the offended. In this instance the Gibeonites refused the payment of a ransom price and disallowed just any Israelite's dying as a substitute or appeasement (21:4). They demanded that seven of Saul's descendants be delivered to them for execution. The execution was to take the form of hanging (21:6). By hanging, they did not mean with a rope from a tree, but instead, they intended to impale their victims on a stake. To add to the shame, the impaled bodies of the sons of Saul would be displayed in Saul's home town of Gibeah.

David followed the instructions of the Gibeonites and found seven descendants of Saul—two sons of Rizpah, Saul's concubine (cf. II Samuel 3:7), and five sons of Adriel, the husband of Merab, Saul's oldest daughter (21:8; cf. I Samuel 18:19). The mention of

Michal in verse eight may be explained by inferring that Merab had died and Michal, who was childless (6:23), reared these children for her sister. It should also be noted that Mephibosheth was excluded from the death sentence because of David's vow to Jonathan (21:7). These seven were handed over to the men of Gibeon, who impaled them during the first days of barley harvest (21:9). From Leviticus 23 we learn that the barley harvest came after the Passover and Feast of Unleavened Bread. Therefore, according to our calendar, these men were killed about the middle of April.

The Vigilance of Rizpah (21:10-14)

Although there was nothing she could do to rescue her sons, Rizpah could not endure the thought of her slain sons becoming emaciated and being devoured by scavengers. Taking the sackcloth of mourning, Rizpah made herself a small tent upon the rocks where the corpses of her sons stood exposed (21:10). There she remained *"until water dropped upon them out of heaven."* This statement reveals two pertinent facts. First, the drought and famine were ended. Justice had been performed. The atonement was received. Second, we learn when Rizpah's vigil was complete. The dropping of the rain was a sign of the beginning of the early rains in the fall. These began around the middle of October.

Let's piece together the scene before us. Rizpah is now an elderly lady at least in her sixties, but probably much older. For six months she bore the intense heat and dry weather while repelling the wild animals that stalked the bodies of her sons. She must have experienced many sleepless nights as sounds out of the darkness haunted her. Only a broken heart of a mother could be so selfless in its love and devotion.

Such faithfulness could not go unnoticed. An observer reported the story to King David, who was moved by what he heard (21:11). Enough was enough. The punishment was sufficient. From Jabesh-gilead David brought the bones of Saul and Jonathan that had been buried there (21:12; cf. I Samuel 31:12-13). Then he took the bones of Rizpah's sons and the other five descendants of Saul and buried them all honorably in the tomb of Kish in Zelah of the country of Benjamin (21:13-14). God was pleased in what had been done, and He restored His blessings upon Israel.

The Valiance of David's Men (21:15-22)

David grew older, but his days were not peaceful. The old nemesis of the Philistine nation reared again her ugly head in opposition to her neighbor. David led his men into battle as was his custom even though he was at least sixty-five years old. However, time had taken its toll; and in the thick of the battle, David became weary (21:15). Over him stood a giant by the name of Ishbi-benob with drawn sword glistening in the sun and a seven-to-eight-pound spear poised at his side. The victor paused to relish the triumph over his victim. It would be interesting to know what went through David's mind in that moment. He might have wondered where that man was who always wanted to cut off someone's head.

Before Ishbi-benob could deal his death blow, Abishai came to David's aid and killed the giant (21:17). For all practical purposes, the fighting was over, and the men of Israel gathered around their aging king. Everyone knew the implications of what had happened. David must never again venture out into the field of battle. The risks were too high. David's leadership was too valuable to place him in a vulnerable position. No doubt a few tears were shed, and the hearts of the men were heavy.

Soon afterwards the Philistines made another attack with a new champion—Saph, the giant. The armies met at Gob (probably on the outskirts of Gath), and Sibbechai the Hushathite bested the giant (21:18). A second conflict arose at Gob involving a giant from Gath (21:19). First Chronicles 20:5 informs us that he was the brother of Goliath, called Lahmi. But he, too, was slain by one of David's men, Elhanan. One final battle is mentioned as occurring in Gath. The Philistine fighter is not named. He is described as *"a man of great stature that had on every hand six fingers, and on every foot six toes" (21:20).* This giant may well have been the greatest threat to Israel. As did his predecessor Goliath, this champion *"defied Israel" (21:22),* which means he taunted, insulted, and cast scorn upon the people of God. When the situation looked bleak, Jonathan, whose uncle was David, stepped forward to fight the giant. Jonathan won.

Of the four men named who conquered the giants, only one is familiar—Abishai. The others were little-known servants of David, but the meaning of their names gives us insight into their character and source of strength. *Sibbechai* means "Jehovah is intervening." *Elhanan* means "God is gracious." *Jonathan* means "Jehovah has given." Is it any wonder that they were successful?

Four giants are pictured in this passage, but in the overall context I really see only two. The first "giant" is Rizpah, who had "the heart of a mother that reproduced compassion." Society was cruel, cold, and heartless. Everyone was looking out for Number One, trying to make ends meet. Yet Rizpah was not hardened even in her old age. Her tenderness in time of tribulation touched the heart of the king and provoked him to deeds of compassion. Her affection makes her a giant among men—no doubt about it.

The other "giant" in this story is David, who exemplified "the life of a man who reproduced courage." A half century earlier there had been no one in Israel willing to face the giants (cf. I Samuel 17). A shepherd boy who had little experience but great faith in God left his mark on history by boldly walking into the valley of the shadow of death to meet Goliath. Now near the end of David's life he could no longer physically engage the giants. But David's consistent life of faith and courage also left its mark on men. Instead of no one willing to fight the giants, David reproduced a generation of giant killers.

Rizpah and David offer two valuable commodities for the children of God today—compassion and courage. We dare not develop one without the other. Both are needed in abundance in our nation, our churches, and our homes. And both are needed in balance.

TIMELESS TRUTHS FOR TODAY

1. A heart of compassion will reproduce compassion.

2. A life of courage will reproduce courage.

Chapter 25

A Song of Praise
from Feeble Lips
II Samuel 22:1-51

Exhausted from the intense fighting, a mighty warrior collapsed in fatigue. A giant of a man stood over his would-be victim, savoring the moment of the approaching death of his foe. Miraculously, a faithful friend of the fallen soldier came to the rescue. But the interlude that followed was far from jubilant. Sure, there was a sense of thankfulness that the friend was safe, but there lingered the memory of what might have been.

The story, of course, is of David's encounter with the Philistine Ishbi-benob (II Samuel 21:15). For decades David had been the commander-in-chief on the field of battle. His military leadership in combat had set the standard for his men. David had lived a full, rich life. But life does not go on forever. From our perspective we know that within five years he would be dead. Those last years could not be spent in fighting. The

close call with Ishbi-benob proved that only too well.
The remainder of David's days must be lived within the
safe confines of Jerusalem. David's lifestyle was under-
going change.

How do you face change? How do you respond when
you hear the words, "You can't do that any more;
you're not the same as you once were; why don't you
sit back and let us worry about the problems"? Life was
passing David by. Failure became more frequent.
Fatigue became more extreme. Fears became more
threatening. David's reaction is preserved in Second
Samuel's twenty-second chapter. You might expect to
find bitterness, resistance, discouragement, or despair.
David framed his thoughts in a poem—a song, if you
please. The song is not a dirge in minor key. It is a
sweet melody of thanksgiving and praise as an old man
reminisces his experiences in life and his fellowship
with God. Let's take a journey into David's head and
heart as he reveals his emotions with pen and ink.

Severe Problems Examined (22:1-19)

You cannot walk life's road without confronting
some problems along the way. David's life was no
exception. The major theme of the first section of this
song seems to be David's problems. With skillful touch
David paints three pictures of his varied trials.

First, he tells how he was terrorized by his fears.
*"When the waves of death compassed me, the floods of ungodly men
made me afraid" (22:5).* His description of the *"waves of
death"* is noteworthy. David chose a word for *"wave"* that
means "to break in pieces." This is amplified by the verb
"compassed," which means "to surround." The image
being portrayed is a lonely character out on the
storming sea. There is a threat on every hand of death.

You brace yourself for a blast from one side, and suddenly you are struck by a wall of water from the other side. Perhaps David recalled how, when he ran from the assaults of Saul, he thought he had found refuge in the town of Keilah (I Samuel 23), which he had delivered from the oppression of the Philistines. Surely they would provide him with safe asylum. Yet they were ready to betray him into the hands of Saul. David was overwhelmed by the waves of disloyalty.

Second, David remembered how he had become immobilized by his failures. He wrote, *"The sorrows of hell compassed me about; the snares of death prevented me; In my distress I called upon the Lord" (22:6, 7)*. Here he portrays himself as being bound up by cords or ropes. (The word *"sorrows"* in the KJV is actually the Hebrew word meaning "cord or rope.") The cords compassed (literally "went around") him. He was tied up. Then he spoke of *"the snares of death which prevented"* him. *"Prevent"* means to confront, while the word *"snare"* pictures for us a trap. David was admitting that he faced daily traps that would have negated his usefulness. His sensual desires, especially the episode with Bathsheba, had ensnared and enslaved him. How often have your past failures immobilized you for effective service?

The third problem was that David was victimized by his foes. David's enemies are referred to many times in this chapter. Often they took advantage of David when he was weak. For instance, he stated, *"They prevented me in the day of my calamity: but the Lord was my stay" (22:19)*. The idea behind the term *"calamity"* is a disaster or downfall. In those times when David nearly fell under the barrage of his enemies, God was his stay. The Hebrew word for *"stay"* comes from a verb meaning "to lean on." In the day of calamity when David was falling, David learned to lean on God. David learned to lean on

God when he faced Goliath (I Samuel 17:45-47), when he ran from Saul (I Samuel 23:13-16), when he had lost a child in death (II Samuel 12:19-23), and when he was driven from his own kingdom by Absalom (II Samuel 15:25-26). God is a strong support when life tries to knock us down.

Sterling Character Extolled (22:20-30)

Even in all of his difficulties, David had one thing going for him. He was a man after God's own heart (I Samuel 13:14). Four qualities in David's character are extolled in this psalm.

1. Personal Integrity. *"He delivered me, because he delighted in me"* (22:20). *"Delight"* means to favor greatly because of some inner quality. David had invited God to examine his heart (II Samuel 15:25-26; cf. Psalm 19:14; 139:23-24), and the Lord had found him "delightful." God delivered David as a reward for his integrity.

2. Biblical Priority. *"The Lord rewarded me according to my righteousness"* (22:21). Here righteousness speaks of a conformity to an ethical or moral standard. David's life was characterized by an adherence to the standards and laws of God. *"For all his judgments were before me"* (22:23). In this verse *"judgments"* refers to God's revealed Word. This Word was *"before"* him. David chose a special word for *"before."* It means "to place prominently or conspicuously before." David had learned the importance of exalting and obeying God's Word.

3. Unquestionable Purity. *"According to the cleanness of my hands hath he recompensed me"* (22:21). Cleanness is

defined as being free or clear of blame. But was David "clean"? He had committed adultery and murder. What about those sins? Long ago David had confessed those, and God had cleansed him. *"Blessed is he whose transgression is forgiven, whose sin is covered. Blessed is the man unto whom the Lord imputeth not iniquity, and in whose spirit there is no guile (Psalm 32:1-2).* David now had a fresh start . . . a second chance . . . a new beginning. He was careful to be clean; and when he failed, he was careful to confess.

4. Humble Maturity. *"I was also upright before him"* (22:24). "To be complete" is the basic meaning behind *"upright."* David was maturing, becoming complete, in his relationship with God. He could have been tempted to be proud, but he remembered, *"And the afflicted people thou wilt save"* (22:28). *"Afflicted"* also could be translated "humble." David knew that his growth must be tempered by humility if he were to enjoy the blessing of God.

And what will God do for the man who possesses personal integrity, Biblical priority, unquestionable purity, and humble maturity?

Supernatural Deliverance Experienced (22:31-46)

God saw David's dilemma, and he saw David's character. Consequently he rewarded him with deliverance. Earlier in the chapter David described one way God had helped him (22:7-18). The Lord is pictured with his angels, riding on the wind, exercising judgment upon David's enemies. The brilliance of God's holiness shines out of the dark clouds; and lightning, like arrows, is hurled against the foes. God speaks and the sins are washed away. He rebukes and the earth is laid bare. What an awesome picture of our delivering God!

However, God did not do everything for David. Instead, the Lord gave David strength (22:33) and training (22:35) so that the enemy could be defeated. In verses thirty-eight through forty-four, a description is given of how David triumphed over his adversaries through the power of God. Look at the words David chooses to speak of his conquests—*"pursued," "destroyed," "consumed," "wounded," "fallen," "subdued," "beat," "stamp," "spread,"* and *"delivered."* Also, in those seven verses David used the pronoun *"I"* six times to indicate what he had done, but used *"thou"* of God five times to show God's hand in the deliverance. Here then is the unique balance of how we can overcome our enemies and problems. We do not win battles by piously sitting back and letting God do it. Nor can we win battles in our own strength. We are to do our part (faithful obedience), and God will do His part (enabling power).

Sincere Praise Expressed (22:47-51)

The song begins and ends with a familiar refrain— praise to God. Several titles are used of God throughout the psalm: *"my rock," "my shield," "the horn of salvation," "my refuge," "my saviour," "my stay," "a buckler," "my lamp," "my strength," "the tower of salvation."* From these names I have chosen four which convey the basic idea of what God intends to do for us.

1. He is our support when we are falling. The enemies of David sought to afflict him in his calamity or downfall. God was his stay, his support, his staff to lean on to keep from falling (22:19). God also *"enlarged* [his] *steps . . . so that* [his] *feet did not slip"* (22:37).

The Lord does not want His children to stumble and fall when the way is rough.

2. He is our shelter when we are fearful. The terms *"buckler"* and *"shield"* appearing in this passage refer to a small round shield used to cover up when the blows of the enemy's sword came down against his victim. This shield was a lifesaver. David said, *"He* [God] *is a buckler to all them that trust in him" (22:31).* This word for *"trust"* means "to seek refuge, to flee for protection." It speaks of a sudden or abrupt action taken because of approaching danger. Who can doubt that we all face potential threats from the enemy daily? When the persecution and pressure come, the Lord invites us to flee quickly to Him. He will shelter us from the attacks.

3. He is our strength when we are frail. *"God is my strength and power: and he maketh my way perfect (22:33).* At times the temptations become strong and we become weak. The tendency is to "give-in." But God can enable and empower us to stand against the temptation.

4. He is our song when we are faint. David had *"waxed faint" (21:15).* Battle fatigue had left him weary. Change had to take place. There was no bitterness— only a song (22:1). As he reflected on the past and present goodness of God, he could say, *"I will give thanks."* How grateful are you for God's abundant grace you have experienced through the years?

Our God is our support, our shelter, our strength, and our song. Such realization should drive us to proclaim, *"The Lord liveth; and blessed be my rock; and exalted be the God of the rock of my salvation" (22:47).*

TIMELESS TRUTHS FOR TODAY

1. The Lord is our support when we are falling.

2. The Lord is our shelter when we are fearful.

3. The Lord is our strength when we are frail.

4. The Lord is our song when we are faint.

Chapter 26

David's Hall of Heroes
II Samuel 23:1-39

In February of 1945, Joseph Goebbels, one of the original Nazi leaders, predicted that the Russians would drop "an iron curtain" between their occupied lands and the western nations. This prediction was made to stun the United States and Great Britain and perhaps to buy time for Germany to regroup. On May 1, 1945, Goebbels realized the futility of his Nazi cause and killed himself. During that same month Winston Churchill sent a top-secret telegram to President Truman in which he used the phrase, "iron curtain." Ten months after the war Churchill publicly spoke of the dangers facing the future of the world. One of the greatest dangers he mentioned was the "iron curtain." History has proved the prophecy of Goebbels and Churchill to be true. These men, not prophets in the true sense of the word, were simply able to discern the times and foresee the effects of present events.

When we look into the prophecies of God's Word, we find another story. The prophets of the Bible are not merely giving their perspective. They spoke under divine inspiration and were allowed to view events that would be fulfilled centuries later. One of these prophets was a king by the name of David, who died around 970 B.C., but who wrote of a day yet future when an "iron curtain" would be replaced by a "rod of iron."

Prophetic Poetry (23:1-7)

The chapter begins with the statement: *"Now these be the last words of David" (23:1).* This refers to the last formal or public proclamation made by the king. His words were divinely inspired as evidenced by the use of the Hebrew word *neʾum* (KJV *"said," v. 1*), which was employed exclusively of divine speaking. Inspiration is further emphasized in verses two and three, *"The Spirit of the Lord spake by me, and his word was in my tongue. The God of Israel said, the Rock of Israel spake to me."* Thus David became a vehicle for the transmission of a prophetic revelation of future events. The literary form in the original is poetic, which is not surprising since David is labeled *"the sweet psalmist of Israel" (23:1).*

David, in the spirit, foresaw an individual who would rule in righteousness (KJV *"just"*) and in the fear of God (23:3). Using a natural phenomenon to describe that reign, David revealed that this person would radiate light like the brilliance of the sunrise on a cloudless day (23:4). The picture is further enhanced by an allusion to the growth of new grass which is produced by the sunshine after a nourishing rain. Who is the identity of this individual? To what event does the prophet point? It is clear from verse five that we are viewing the

fulfillment of the *"everlasting covenant"* that was made
with David (cf. II Samuel 7:8-16). The individual
spoken of is Jesus Christ, who will establish a literal
kingdom on the earth. Jeremiah wrote, *"In those days, and
at that time, will I cause the Branch of righteousness to grow up
unto David; and he shall execute judgment and righteousness in the
land" (Jeremiah 33:15).* Another prophet recorded, *"But
unto you that fear my name shall the Sun of righteousness arise
with healing in his wings" (Malachi 4:2).* Isaiah, perhaps the
greatest of all prophets, looked forward to Christ's
kingdom, saying, *"And there shall come forth a rod out of the
stem of Jesse, and a Branch shall grow out of his roots . . . with
righteousness shall he judge . . . and righteousness shall be the
girdle of his loins" (Isaiah 11:1, 4, 5).* It is Christ who is the
righteous Branch and the Sun of Righteousness who
will rule. The millennial kingdom will dawn as a
"morning without clouds" (23:4). The powers of darkness
will be dispelled. As thorns the wicked will be gathered
and burned (23:6, 7; cf. Revelation 19:17-21; Matthew
25:31-46). In that day *"the earth shall be filled with the
knowledge of the glory of the Lord, as the waters cover the sea"
(Habakkuk 2:14).* What a day that will be!

As we prepare for that day, we may gather this
practical advice from David's poetry. To the man who
allows the Lord to rule in his heart, who builds
righteousness (i.e., conformity to God's standards) in
his life, and who fears God in his spirit, the Lord will
radiate His glory through him to the world. Through
the water of the Word and the sunshine of His presence, God will cause us to grow even as the *"tender grass
. . . after rain."* Why wait for the blessings?

Heroic Bravery (23:8-39)

The mood of the passage passes from pen to sword as

the author moves from prophetic words to heroic deeds. A list of David's mighty men and a concise collection of their exploits preserve for us the spirit of bravery that possessed this select company. First, however, a brief synopsis of David's military organization would be in order.

Each month a fresh corps of twenty-four thousand men were appointed to serve and protect their nation (I Chronicles 27:1). This meant that David had available to him a standing army of 288,000 soldiers who could be called up in case of an emergency. David was also surrounded by a personal bodyguard—the Cherethites and the Pelethites (II Samuel 8:18). These men were probably mercenaries of Grecian or Philistine origin. Their respective names indicate that they were executioners and couriers for the king. A final category can be designated as David's "special force." Their beginning was inauspicious. Four hundred men who were *in distress . . . in debt . . . and discontented"* huddled together in a dark cave called Adullam (I Samuel 22:2). The prospects of molding a loyal band of fighters from this motley crew appeared bleak. Yet they stuck with David through his lean and fugitive years. The number even grew to six hundred (I Samuel 27:2). When David was anointed as king in Hebron, they were with him (II Samuel 2:1-3). They faithfully stood by him during the early Philistine conflicts near Jerusalem (II Samuel 5), through the subtle take-over by Absalom (II Samuel 15:18; 16:6), and through the revolt of Sheba (II Samuel 20:7). From this nucleus came David's mighty men, also called *"the thirty" (23:13).* Some have suggested that *"the thirty"* were leaders of divisions of twenty men each from the 600. This is highly likely. The list given in II Samuel 23 obviously contains more than thirty names, since when one died, he was replaced by another.

Several special leaders are mentioned by name along with some outstanding feats. Three men were held in high esteem—Jashobeam (or Adino), Eleazar, and Shammah. Jashobeam is noted for his success in defeating and killing eight hundred men in one battle (23:8). This victory earned for him the title "chief of the captains."

Eleazar was a soldier who refused to quit. On one occasion the Philistines had fought the Israelites to the point of retreat. While the armies of Israel scampered to the hills for safety, Eleazar stood his ground and taunted the enemy (23:9). God honored the courage of this man and gave him the stamina to fight. By the end of the day, Eleazar was so weary that *"his hand clave unto the sword" (23:10).* His fellow soldiers could hardly believe their eyes. In jubilation they returned to strip the dead and take the spoil.

The third major character remembered is Shammah. Harvest time was approaching, and the Philistines were hoping to invade Israel and take the Jewish crops. The confrontation took place in *"a place of ground full of lentiles" (23:11)* or more simply, a pea patch. The Jews ran when they saw the mighty Philistines, but not Shammah. He set himself with firm resolution right in the middle of that piece of ground and refused to budge. Some time later after a hard-fought battle, Shammah remained erect in the field where the Philistines had fallen. Again *"the Lord wrought a great victory" (23:12).*

On another occasion earlier in David's career, he and his men were holding up in the cave of Adullam. David had been gone from Bethlehem, his home, for a long time; and during his absence the Philistines had made the town a garrison (23:14). Experiencing a touch of homesickness, David pined, "Boy, what I wouldn't give for a drink of water from the well of Bethlehem right now" (cf. 23:15). He had often stopped at that well for a cool drink on a hot day. Perhaps he had spent many hours there as he carefully watered his father's sheep. He longed for a reminder of more peaceful, happy days. Life had become complicated, and David was discouraged. Three of David's men heard about the desire of their leader and determined to fulfill the wish, regardless of the cost. Secretly they made their way to the enemy camp at Bethlehem, fought through enemy lines, retrieved the water, and returned to Adullam (23:16). Those brave troops could not have anticipated what would take place next. Rather than allowing himself the luxury of drinking the water, David did a noble thing. He poured the water out before the Lord as an offering because sacrifice demands sacrifice (23:16). The water was representative of the blood of the three men who had risked their lives for David (23:17). David felt himself unworthy of such devotion and directed the loyalty of his men to God instead. How careful leaders must be in directing attention from themselves and in focusing upon being servants of God.

The next hero listed is Abishai (23:18, 19). He must have been one of the three who broke through the line at Bethlehem and brought back the water for David (23:18b). Abishai is well known to us as the brother of Joab, and one of David's loyal men. Although Abishai's exploits were many, one earned him the reputation of being a mighty man. In one engagement Abishai killed three hundred men by himself. Such ability had propelled him into leadership position during various wars (cf. II Samuel 10:10; 18:2; 20:6).

Benaiah had a family heritage of bravery. His ancestors were valiant men (23:20). And Benaiah lived up to the family name. Once he killed two *"lionlike men of Moab"* in combat. At another time he matched up against a muscular Egyptian, who was seven and one-half feet tall (I Chronicles 11:23). The Egyptian had a spear, while Benaiah was armed with a club. But Benaiah *"plucked the spear out of the Egyptian's hand, and slew him with his own spear" (23:21).* The word *"plucked"* indicates a violent seizure or tearing away. Benaiah was skilled in hand-to-hand combat, one-on-one encounter. An interesting sidelight is also given about him. It happened on a snowy day in the high country of Israel. As Benaiah was walking along the hills, he heard the roar of a lion that had fallen into a pit. Unbelievably, he went down into that pit and took on the lion—and won! (I would love to have more details about that story.) Judging from these acts, it is not surprising that Benaiah was chosen to be head of David's personal bodyguard (II Samuel 8:18). Later he became captain over all of the armies of Israel under Solomon (I Kings 2:35).

The remainder of the chapter only lists the names of the other mighty men. Undoubtedly, each has his own "war stories" of courage and bravery. First Chronicles reveals that the one goal of these men was to make David king; but by so doing, they strengthened themselves (I Chronicles 11:10). How instructive! The way to success is by serving others. For the Christian the teaching is plain. Consume yourself in establishing Christ's kingdom and you, too, will be established.

Thirty-seven men are eulogized in this chapter. Why? What practical lesson can we learn from their examples? The common denominator of these men is that they stood. They stood in spite of the opposition (23:8, 9, 11, 18, 20, 21). Out-numbered, out-muscled, out-maneuvered—but they stood. They stood in spite of the exhaustion (23:9, 10). Weary and worn, frightened and fatigued—but they did not quit. They stood in spite of the confusion (23:9, 11). When everyone else ran helter-skelter, these men stood their ground. And because they stood, *"the Lord wrought a great victory"* (23:10, 12).

Whether we like it or not, we are in a fight. The opposition is strong; the exhaustion is severe; the confusion is great. But we are encouraged, *"Be strong in the Lord, and in the power of his might. Put on the whole armour of God, that ye may be able to stand against the wiles of the devil . . . Wherefore take unto you the whole armour of God, that ye may be able to withstand in the evil day, and having done all, to stand. Stand therefore"* (Ephesians 6:10, 11, 13, 14). Stand against . . . withstand . . . stand . . . stand therefore. Our orders are clear. May our courage be strong.

TIMELESS TRUTHS FOR TODAY

---

1. **Stand for Christ in spite of the opposition.**

2. **Stand for Christ in spite of the exhaustion.**

3. **Stand for Christ in spite of the confusion.**

Chapter 27

The High Price of Pride
II Samuel 24:1-25

John Boys, a Puritan writer from another century, penned these words, "As death is the last enemy; so pride the last sin that shall be destroyed in us." David could offer a hearty "Amen" to the truth of that statement. Just when the problems and tensions of David's twilight years seemed to be lessening, pride prompted David to make a serious blunder. Soon David would experience the results of pride of which his son later wrote: *"Pride goeth before destruction, and an haughty spirit before a fall" (Proverbs 16:18).*

The Numbering of the People (24:1-10)

The chapter opens with a revelation that someone *"moved David . . . to say, Go, number Israel and Judah" (24:1).* This "someone" has been identified as Jehovah by many. The Chronicler, however, provides for us a

221

more complete picture. *"And Satan stood up against Israel, and provoked David to number Israel" (I Chronicles 21:1).* Since no action against God's children can be taken without God's approval (cf. Job 1:6-12), God allowed the testing to come. When David failed the test, yielding to Satan's provocation, *"the anger of the Lord was kindled" (24:1).* And what was the sin that caused heaven's anger to burn? Was it the taking of a census? Certainly not, because guidelines for a census had been previously given (cf. Exodus 30:12). Consider, also, that Moses himself numbered the people of Israel twice according to God's command (Numbers 1, 26). The sin must be found in David's motives. Even the brutish Joab recognized David's wrong attitudes. When the captain was told to travel from Dan to Beer-sheba to number the people, he heard David say, *"Number ye the people, that I may know the number of the people" (24:2).* No war was impending. No threat forced the king to take a census. Pure and simple, David wanted to boast in the military strength he had attained.

Joab's protest was polite but pointed (24:3). His prayer was that God might multiply David's servants *"an hundredfold."* But he questioned David's motives by asking, *"Why doth my lord the king delight in this thing?"* Joab went so far as to accuse David of causing the people to sin (I Chronicles 21:3). However, David would not listen to the warnings from his friend; *"the king's word prevailed" (24:4).* Clearly, attitudes of pride, selfishness, insensitivity, and stubbornness are evident in David's words and actions.

Reluctantly and half-heartedly, Joab and his captains began the census (24:4). During the next nine months and twenty days, these men journeyed east, north, west, and south through the cities of Israel and her vassal cities in order to determine the number of

fighting men available (24:5-8). The count given to
David was listed under the two major divisions of the
nation. The northern tribes (i.e., Israel) accounted for
eight hundred thousand warriors, which probably did
not include the standing army of nearly three hundred
thousand (cf. I Chronicles 27:1ff). These additional
troops were included in the final total mentioned in I
Chronicles 21:5. The tribe of Judah was represented by
a half million soldiers. The sum of David's armies was
over one million and six hundred thousand, which did
not take into consideration the men of Levi or
Benjamin. Joab failed to complete the census because
"the king's word was abominable to him" *(I Chronicles 21:6).*
Joab found it impossible to be obedient to royal commands that he knew to be contrary to God's commands.

When the numbering was finished, God made known
His displeasure over the incident by *"smiting"* Israel (I
Chronicles 21:7). Whatever this initial affliction was,
we are not told; but it did drive David to confess his sin
(24:10). Not only did David see his sin as great, but he
recognized it as foolish. (The Hebrew word for *"foolish"*
expresses the sense of lacking moral or spiritual judgment.) The sincere prayer of the king was that God
might remove the guilt and punishment (KJV *"iniquity"*)
of this sin.

The Suffering of the People (24:11-17)

The next morning the Lord summoned an old
prophet by the name of Gad to deliver a message to
David. Gad had been with David since the days of
hiding in the cave of Adullam (I Samuel 22:5), and had
proved himself a true prophet and faithful friend. But
the message on the prophet's lips was one of judgment,
not grace. David was given the responsibility of

choosing the punishment that would fall on his people. The choices included an extended famine lasting three years (cf. I Chronicles 21:12), three months of defeat before Israel's enemies, or three days of plague over the nation (24:13). Some choices! David cried, *"I am in a great strait" (24:14)*, which is the same as saying, "I'm in a bind." What would you have chosen?

David's reasoning went something like this. "Three years is a long time. The people will grow weary and be constantly reminded of my failure. Besides, we have just recently come out of a three-year famine (21:1), and the people can't take any more. To fall into the hands of the enemy would be humiliating and brutal. My only choice is to accept the three days of plague, and trust God will be merciful." Therefore he told Gad, *"Let us fall now into the hand of the Lord; for his mercies are great: and let me not fall into the hand of man" (24:14).* Other meanings for *"mercy"* include "to love deeply, to be compassionate." The word usually refers to a deep love that a superior has for an inferior. David hoped that the Lord would consider his weakness and restrain His hand in love. It is interesting that David did not desire to put his fate in the hands of men. He recognized that God deals far more justly and mercifully than do men. Why do men insist on cruel treatment of each other? Why do we fail to forgive and show mercy? Why must we "kick" others when they are down? David was wise in throwing himself and his people upon the mercy of God.

However, in this case the judgment of God was swift and devastating. No part of the land was exempt. From Dan to Beer-sheba the shadows of death engulfed the lives of seventy thousand Israelites (24:15). The instrument of God's judgment was an angel who now approached the city of Jerusalem with drawn sword ready to destroy more lives. David, in the meantime, along with the elders of Israel, had donned sackcloth as a symbol of repentance (I Chronicles 21:16). Perhaps this act was one of the factors that prompted the Lord to stay momentarily the hand of His destroying angel (II Samuel 24:16). The word *"stay"* means "to sink down, to let drop." The sword is still unsheathed, but now it rests by the angel's side.

As the angel stood near the threshingfloor of Araunah (or Ornan), David prayed again to God: *"Lo, I have sinned, and I have done wickedly: but these sheep, what have they done? let thine hand, I pray thee, be against me, and against my father's house" (24:17).* I admire those words! A simple confession: *"I have sinned."* A logical question: *"But these sheep, what have they done?"* A responsible reaction: *"Let thine hand, I pray thee, be against me."* But God's holiness demands restitution for sin. What could be done to satisfy a just God?

The Offering for the People (24:18-25)

There was a way out. The angel instructed Gad to tell David to build an altar on the threshingfloor of Araunah (24:18). Since David did not own that property, he must purchase it from Araunah. As David climbed the hill to the threshingfloor, Araunah and his four sons were threshing and storing grain (I Chronicles 21:20). Before Araunah and his boys saw David coming, they saw the angel with a drawn sword. The sons immediately hid themselves for fear of death. At that moment David approached, and Araunah went out to meet him (24:20). When asked why he had come, David replied, *"To buy the threshingfloor of thee, to build an altar unto the Lord, that the plague may be stayed from the people" (24:21).* Araunah realized the seriousness of the situation and responded with an offer to *"give it all"* (I Chronicles 21:23). Araunah was willing to do anything he could to place David and the people in a position of favor with God (24:23). His willingness to sacrifice for others is an outstanding example of good stewardship. Araunah did not selfishly cling to his land. He was ready to give to meet needs.

David must have been humbled by the gracious offer; but he refused it, saying, *"Nay; but I will surely buy it of thee at a price: neither will I offer burnt offerings unto the Lord my God of that which doth cost me nothing"* (24:24). David knew he must "pay the price" for his sin. How could he truly sacrifice if he himself had made no "sacrifice"? The threshingfloor was purchased for fifty shekels. The purchase price for the entire property (about thirty-five acres) was six hundred shekels of gold, which is roughly equivalent to three hundred ounces of gold (I Chronicles 21:25).

After David prepared the altar and provided the burnt and peace offerings, God demonstrated His approval by sending fire from heaven to consume the offerings (I Chronicles 21:26). The Lord also commanded His angel to *"put up his sword again into the sheath"* (I Chronicles 21:27). With that, everyone gave a sigh of relief. David continued to offer sacrifices of praise and may have journeyed to Gibeon to make offerings at the tabernacle which Moses had built (I Chronicles 21:28-30). God's wrath had been stayed. The crisis was over. And David had come a long way in conquering his pride.

Let's summarize this incident briefly. First, David yielded to temptation foolishly (24:10). He knew to number the people was wrong. Joab and others gave him strong warnings, but David refused to listen and foolishly sinned. How much like today's Christian that is. Our problem is not so much in knowing what is right and wrong; it is in the doing of right and refraining from wrong. Second, David accepted the responsibility completely (24:10, 17). David did not try to hide his sin or pass the buck. He took the blame and was willing to accept the punishment. Third, David looked for mercy prayerfully (24:13, 17). Even though he had done wrong, David did not sit back. He humbled himself and threw himself upon God's mercy, earnestly praying for forgiveness. Yet when today's Christian is confronted with his failures, he hesitates to confess and forsake his sins. Fourth, David obeyed God quickly (24:19). God heard David's prayer and gave him instructions to go and build an altar. A delay in obedience could have meant further sorrow and destruction. Fifth, David offered restitution sacrificially (24:24). David's sin cost him dearly, but the peace that came was worth every penny. His conscience was clear. His account was clean.

Before we pass from this scene, we should not fail to make the following observation. The threshingfloor of Araunah has an auspicious history. In the book of Genesis, we read of this place as Mount Moriah, where Abraham brought Isaac to be offered (Genesis 22:2). Abraham renamed the location *"Jehovah-jireh,"* meaning "the Lord will provide" (Genesis 22:14). This was a prophetic hint of what would one day happen on this mount. After David purchased this site, he proclaimed it as *"the house of the Lord God" (I Chronicles 22:1).* Not long afterward, Solomon would build a glorious temple on that spot (II Chronicles 3:1). But the most significant act that would take place on that mountain would occur approximately one thousand years after David's time. Jesus Christ was crucified on the north extension of Mount Moriah. Where David experienced God's mercy through an offering, we all can taste of God's mercy through the offering of His Son.

My good friend Ron Hamilton wrote the following words in one of his songs. His invitation serves as a fitting conclusion.*

> Look to the cross of the Lamb of God
> Lay all your guilt on Him;
> Freely His life blood He sacrificed,
> Paying the debt of your sin.
>
> *Chorus:*
> Come to the cross upon Calvary,
> Gaze on the scene anew;
> Turn from your sin to the Saviour,
> There Jesus waits for you.

TIMELESS TRUTHS FOR TODAY

When you have yielded to temptation foolishly, take the following steps of action:

1. Accept responsibility completely.

2. Seek for mercy prayerfully.

3. Obey God quickly.

4. Offer restitution sacrificially.

*Copyright 1976 by Musical Ministries. "Come to the Cross," by Ron Hamilton. Used by permission.